SCIENCE WORLD

1

Series Editor:

John Holman

Assessment Editor:

Ken Dobson

Author Team:

Liz Bradley

Ken Dobson

David King

Philip Stone

John Stringer

Charles Tracy

Jane Vellacott

Nelson

Thomas Nelson and Sons Ltd
Nelson House   Mayfield Road
Walton-on-Thames   Surrey
KT12 5PL   UK

51 York Place
Edinburgh
EH1 3JD   UK

Thomas Nelson (Hong Kong) Ltd
Toppan Building 10/F
22A Westlands Road
Quarry Bay   Hong Kong

Thomas Nelson Australia
102 Dodds Street
South Melbourne
Victoria 3205   Australia

Nelson Canada
1120 Birchmount Road
Scarborough   Ontario
M1K 5G4   Canada

© Liz Bradley, Ken Dobson, John
Holman, David King, Philip Stone,
John Stringer, Charles Tracy, Jane
Vellacott, 1993

First published by Thomas Nelson and
Sons Ltd 1993

ISBN 0-17-438414-9

NPN 9 8 7 6 5 4 3 2 1

Acknowledgements

The authors and publishers are grateful to the following for the permission to
use their photographs:

Action Plus: p84, 93; Aerofilms: p52, 122; Allsport: p20, 84, 85, 86,92, 104; Ancient
Art and Architecture: p52; Aviation Photos: p66; BBC: p117, 124; Clive Barda:
p112; Stuart Boreham: p62 (2), 67, 87, 94, 109, 110, 114, 117; Heather
Angel/Biofotos: p24, 32; Bubbles Photo Library: p94; Bridgeman Art Library: p8;
British Coal: p51, 59; J Allan Cash: p56, 57 (2), 65, 73, 76, 82; Bruce Coleman: p21,
51, 73; Simon Collier: p97; Graham Cooper: p113; Department of Antiquity: p52;
Mary Evans Picture Library: p6; Environmental Picture Library: p58, 59; Everest:
p122; Fisons: p3 (26 pictures); Gary Fry: p109; Sally and Richard Greenhill: p46
(2), 97; Health Education: p46; Robert Harding: p34, 60; Phillip Harris: p7; Holt
Studios: p122; Hulton Deutsch: p10, 12, 60, 78; Hutchison Photo Library: p34, 46,
57, 60, 61, 106; Image Bank: p77, 81, 111, 117; Magnum/Chris Steel Perkins: p24;
Marion and Tony Morrison: p24; Network Photographers: p46, 51, 77, 80; NHPA:
p21, 22, 23 (2), 32 (2), 33, 37, 50, 51, 57, 68 (3), 81, 85, 98, 105 (2), 119, 120; Oxford
Scientific Films: p22, 39; Pictor International: p84, 105, 116; QA Photos: p107;
Chris Ridgers Photography: p3, 14, 33, 35, 38, 50, 62, 63, 67, 69, 70, 74, 75 (2), 87,
106, 108, 109, 111, 112, 113; Rex Features: p14; Frank Spooner: p20; Sporting
Pictures: p89; Philip Stone: p58; ZEFA: p42.

Cover photograph by Marty Loken

Illustrations by:
Jane Cope, Ann Gowland, Helen Holroyd, David Holmes, Annabel Milne, Chris
Perry, Michael Salter, Jane Templeman, Ken Vail Graphic Design, David
Williams.

The publishers have made every effort to trace the relevant copyright holders,
but if they have inadvertently omitted any appropriate acknowledgements they
will be pleased to make suitable corrections at the first opportunity.

Contents

TOPIC 1 ■ BEING A SCIENTIST

1.1	Welcome to the science laboratory!	2
1.2	Safety is your concern	4
1.3	Making things look bigger	6
1.4	What is science?	8
1.5	More than a guess	10
1.6	Lighter than air	12
1.7	Is this science?	14
1.8	This is science!	16
Activity	What happens next?	18

TOPIC 2 ■ LOOKING AT LIFE

2.1	What's it like out there?	20
2.2	Survival	22
2.3	A good place to live?	24
2.4	Sort it out	26
2.5	Classification of living things	28
2.6	Living without a backbone	30
2.7	The green kingdom	32
2.8	Looking at variation	34
2.9	Building blocks of life	36
2.10	Being alive	38
2.11	All change	40
2.12	The human life cycle	42
2.13	The future generation	44
2.14	Caring	46
Activity	A homely hedge	48
	Eek! It's a mouse, or is it?	49

TOPIC 3 ■ MATERIALS AND MIXTURES

3.1	Materials around us	50
3.2	Putting materials to work	52
3.3	Materials from the earth	54
3.4	Building materials	56
3.5	Opencast coalmining	58
3.6	Salt	60
3.7	More ways to separate and purify things	62
3.8	Crude oil	64
Activity	Synthetic Materials	66

TOPIC 4 ■ WATER AND THE WEATHER

4.1	Water fit to drink	68
4.2	Solids, liquids and gases	70
4.3	The water cycle	72
4.4	Testing river water samples	74
4.5	Winds	76
4.6	Rain	78
4.7	Our future climate?	80
Activity	Life in a pond	82

TOPIC 5 ■ GETTING GOING

5.1	Sport speeds	84
5.2	Stopping and starting	86
5.3	Faster and faster	88
5.4	Twin forces	90
5.5	Falling	92
5.6	Crashes and bangs	94
5.7	Safety and cars	96
5.8	What is gravity?	98
5.9	Galileo, Newton and gravity	100
Activity	Designing	102

TOPIC 6 ■ LIGHT AND SOUND

6.1	Thunder and lightning	104
6.2	As straight as ...	106
6.3	Lighting things up	108
6.4	Eyes and ears	110
6.5	Making music	112
6.6	Musical tones	114
6.7	Loud and clear	116
6.8	Long distance messages	118
6.9	How does the ear work?	120
6.10	Treat your neighbour as you would like to be treated	122
Activity	Helping the deaf	124

Topic 1 ■ BEING A SCIENTIST

1.1 Welcome to the science laboratory!

Picture 1

Science is an exciting and enjoyable subject. There will be a lot to learn this year – including a lot of new words. You may learn more new words in science than you do in a foreign language! A lot of these new words will be the names of **science apparatus**. So it's just as well if you learn a few right at the start!

Here are some of the apparatus you are going to be using. How many names do you know?

Imagine you are introducing a stranger to the science laboratory.

1 Tell him or her how to light the bunsen burner safely.

2 Tell him or her how to leave the bunsen burner when it's not in use – and why.

3 Tell him or her how to handle, and put down, a hot test tube.

4 Tell him or her how to use a stand and clamp to support a boiling tube.

5 You always wear eye protection when you are doing anything that might be dangerous. Tell him or her why.

6 You match the voltage of bulbs and batteries. Tell him or her why.

Test tube rack

Conical flasks

Stop clock

Spring balance

Evaporating basin

Rubber bung

Hand lens

Voltmeter

Electronic balance

Boss and clamp

Tripod and gauze

Heat proof mat

Spatula

Bunsen burner

Beakers

Apparatus stand

Picture 2 Some laboratory apparatus.

Round-bottomed flask

Picture 1

1.2 Safety is your concern

Keith Thompson is a Safety Officer. He inspects schools. His job is to make sure that everything is as safe as possible. Today he is inspecting a science laboratory like yours.

'This lot look dressed for the job! It's only sensible to dress properly for what we have to do. Loose, floppy coats, hanging ties and long hair are all hazards. Can you think why? A lab coat or an apron can protect your clothes from splashes. The school supplies eye protection to protect your eyes when you are doing experiments.'

'Nice to see all the sports bags tucked safely away under the benches – and nobody eating or drinking. You never know what you might be munching in a science laboratory! And of course, you should **never** taste chemicals – even if you think they are safe!'

'Your teacher will tell you your school's own safety rules. Remember – you should only do experiments that your teacher tells you to do. Trying your own experiments can be dangerous. School laboratories are safe places and accidents are rare. You must always tell your teacher of any accident that takes place, immediately.'

'Fire precautions are vital. You should know all the ways out – they're the first things I look for! The fire escape routes must be kept clear.'

Picture 2

'Do you know your own fire drill? There should be extinguishers and fire blankets in the lab. Do you know why they are different colours? Do you know what they are used for? But it's **not your** job to fight fires! You should know how to go out quickly and without fuss – and where to assemble!'

'Finally, remember to wash your hands – especially after using chemicals, and at the end of every practical lesson.'

Picture 3

QUESTIONS

Imagine you are explaining laboratory safety to a student who will be coming to your school next year. Explain why, when you are doing experiments

1 you should tie back long hair.

2 you should wear eye protection.

3 you should never eat or drink in the science laboratory.

4 you should put your coat and bag away tidily.

5 you should never run in science laboratories.

6 you must wash your hands after practical lessons.

7 you must know the school fire drill.

You could design a safety poster to display in your laboratory.

Picture 4 Here are some of the safety symbols that you need to recognise and understand.

General warning, caution, risk of danger

Caution, risk of electric shock

Caution, harmful and irritant

Hand protection must be worn

Caution, risk of ionising radiation

Caution, risk of explosion

Caution, risk of fire

Eye protection must be worn

Caution, toxic hazard

Caution, corrosive substance

Caution, contains dangerous germs and bacteria

1.3 Making things look bigger

Picture 1 Roger Bacon.

Picture 1 Roger Bacon.

Picture 2 Hand lens.

A School Inspector found a little girl crouching over a flower. 'What are you doing?' he asked. 'I'm using a magic-fying glass!' she said.

The first magnifying glass must have seemed almost magical. Roger Bacon was a Franciscan monk who lived 700 years ago (picture 1). He is believed to have discovered the magnifying glass. His work in a library was interrupted by some craftsmen fitting a new window. Glass at the time often had curved, uneven sides. When he went across to speak to them, he noticed some very large sand grains under a broken piece of glass. He moved the glass to pick up the sand. In fact, the grains were no bigger than any others. He put the piece of glass back. The grains were larger again. The glass was **magnifying** them – making them larger.

Bacon's magnifying glass must have been shaped like the hand lens in picture 2.

The curved sides of the glass bend, or refract the light rays. The picture we see is larger than the thing we are looking at. We call this a **hand lens**.

To see objects clearly using a hand lens:

● keep it clean
● let plenty of light reach the object
● hold the hand lens a fixed distance in front of your eyes, then lift the object towards it
● if you are using a hand lens out of doors, tie it to a string loop round your neck.

The microscope

Roger Bacon was sure that an arrangement of two or more lenses would enlarge things even more. But it was not until some hundreds of years later that lenses were put on either end of a tube, to make a microscope. Picture 3 shows one type of microscope.

Some microscopes have a single set of lenses and prisms and are called **monocular**. Some have a double set, and are called **binocular**.

Monocular microscopes are good for magnifying:

● very tiny objects
● dead animals or parts of animals and plants
● material which has been coloured with stains
● material that has been mounted on a glass slide under a thin glass cover slip, so that light can shine through it.

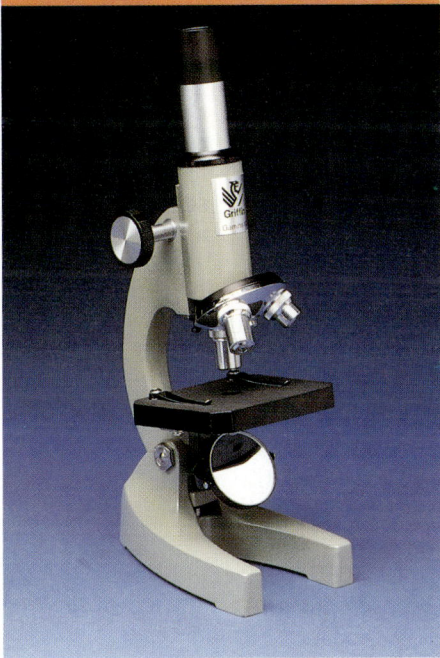
Picture 3 A monocular microscope.

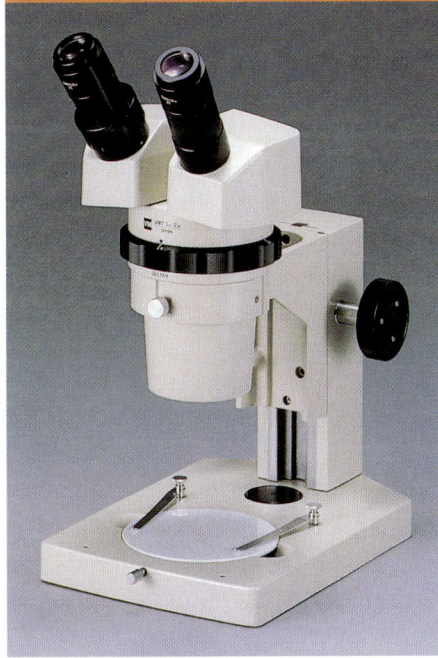
Picture 4 A binocular microscope.

1 In what ways is a microscope better than a hand lens?

2 When is a hand lens more useful than a microscope?

3 When would you use a binocular microscope, rather than a monocular microscope?

4 Look at the three pictures in picture 6. Put them in order of magnification, smallest first. Which gives you the best view of a wasp's head? Can you magnify things too much?

But monocular microscopes don't show things in three dimensions. If you want a 3-D view, you must use a binocular microscope.

To get the best performance from a microscope:

● keep the lenses clean, using only the special tissue.
● make sure that you get the maximum light (from the window or from a lamp) before you start.
● use low power lenses first – they may show you more anyway! Low power lenses are also easier to focus.
● put the slide under the microscope and wind the lens down close to it, while you are watching from the side.
● now look through the lens and wind (or 'rack') the microscope gently up, until the object is in focus.

Picture 6

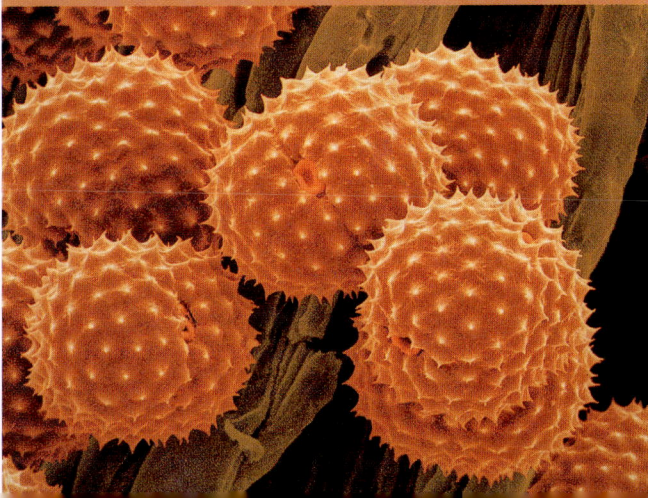
a

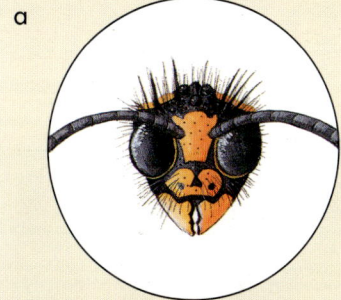
b

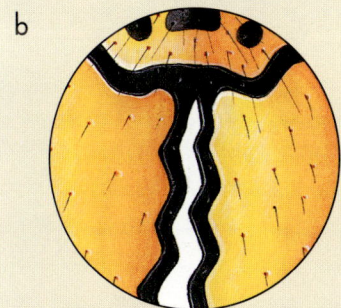
c

Picture 5 A scanning electron micrograph showing pollen grains magnified 1800 times.

1.4 What is science?

Since 1991, the person shown on the £20 note is the scientist Michael Faraday. He was born in 1791 and was the son of a blacksmith.

He began work as a bookbinder covering books with fine leather covers and bindings – but the insides of the books interested him much more than the covers.

When he was 22, he attended the lectures of the great scientist Sir Humphrey Davy. He was so fascinated by these lectures, that he wrote detailed notes on them. Later, he wrote up the notes and bound them into books. Then he presented the books to Davy.

The Royal Institution needed a laboratory assistant. The young Michael Faraday showed all the care and thoroughness they were looking for.

Picture 1 Michael Faraday in 1830 at the age of 39.

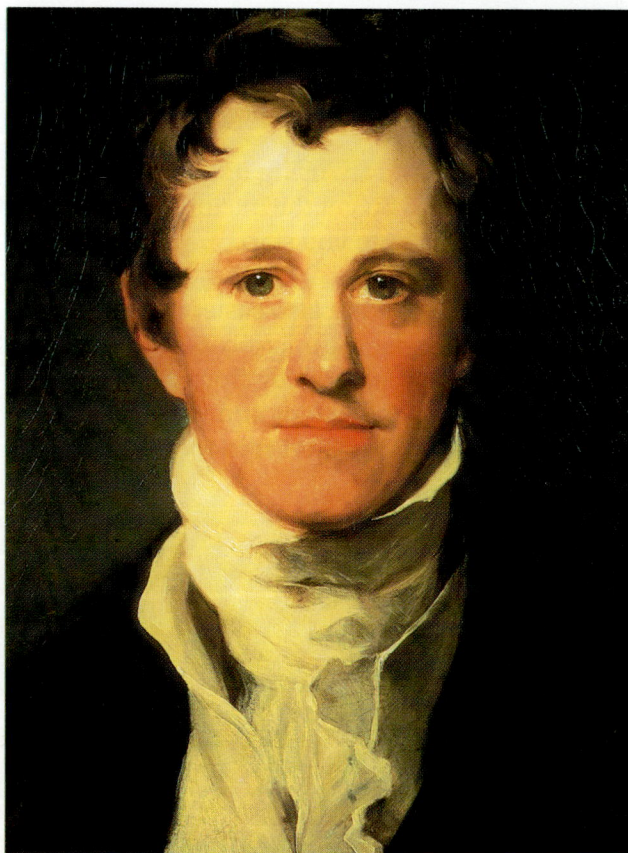

Picture 2 Sir Humphrey Davy in 1797 at the age of 28.

Michael Faraday gave the same care and attention to his observations of a candle (picture 4). He carefully studied how a candle burned and he wrote a whole book on what he observed. He also gave lectures on these observations.

What Faraday did was to look carefully at something that everybody else took for granted. He made careful **observations**.

Making observations is a vital step towards being a good scientist.

Your observations can lead you to make a guess. You may guess at what **you** think is happening. Another name for a guess based on information is a **hypotheses**. You can test your hypotheses. Your test can be called an investigation or an **experiment**.

Picture 3 A typical page from one of Faraday's lecture notebooks.

QUESTIONS

1 Name the five senses you use to make observations.

2 Now list the senses you might use to observe a burning candle.

3 One of your senses is never used in the science laboratory. Which is it, and why not?

4 How do you protect the other four senses when you are doing some science experiments?

Picture 4 Michael Faraday observing and making notes on how a candle burned.

Picture 5 Michael Faraday lecturing to his students.

9

1.5 More than a guess

Often, your observations will lead you to make a **prediction**. A prediction is more than a guess; it's your statement based on close and careful observation.

In 1834, Mary Somerville made a prediction. She made careful observations and calculations on the ways the planets moved. They convinced her that there was another undiscovered planet beyond the planet Uranus.

Mary Somerville's prediction was proved correct twelve years later in 1846, when the planet Neptune was discovered by an astronomer at the Berlin Observatory.

Neptune orbits the Sun at a distance of four and a half thousand million kilometres. It is the third largest of the planets.

When Mary was growing up, in the eighteenth century, she was banned from studying science. Her father believed that it was too difficult for a girl and that it would make her ill. He took her candle away, so that she couldn't read in bed. So Mary memorised mathematical problems and did them in her head.

Picture 1 Mary Somerville.

Picture 2 Planet Neptune.

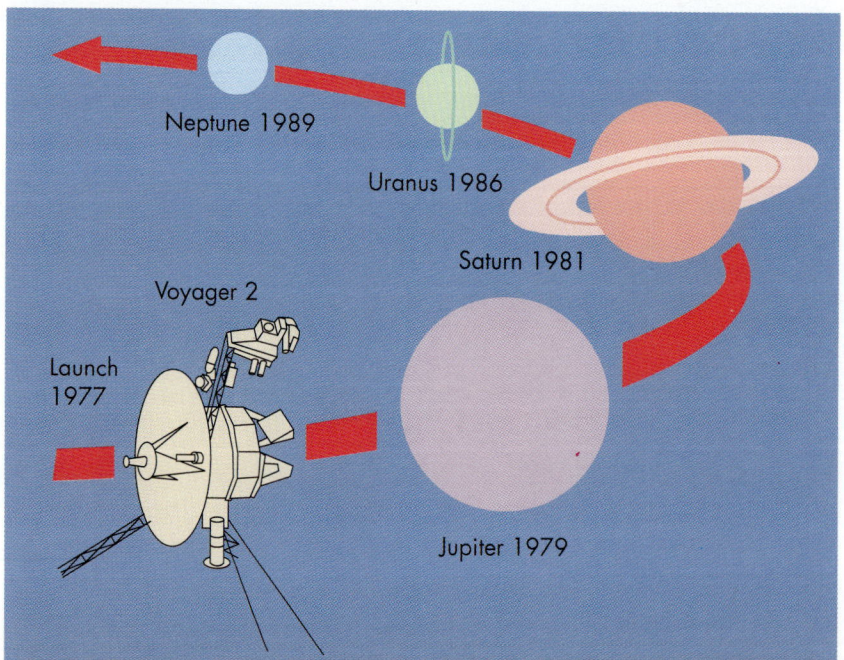

Neptune 1989

Uranus 1986

Saturn 1981

Voyager 2

Launch 1977

Jupiter 1979

Picture 3 A voyage beyond the Solar System of Voyager 2 (launched 1977, never to return).

In 1977, Voyager 2 was launched to look at our Solar System. It passed close to the planet Neptune in 1989. The Voyager project involved a team of scientists – both women and men. Their discoveries will interest scientists in every nation of the World.

Picture 4 Scientists at work.

QUESTIONS

1 Name the smallest and the largest planets in the Solar System.

2 Why do you think Neptune was still undiscovered in Mary's time?

3 Why was Mary brave to tell people about her prediction?

4 Views on women scientists are different now. Name some of the differences from Mary's day.

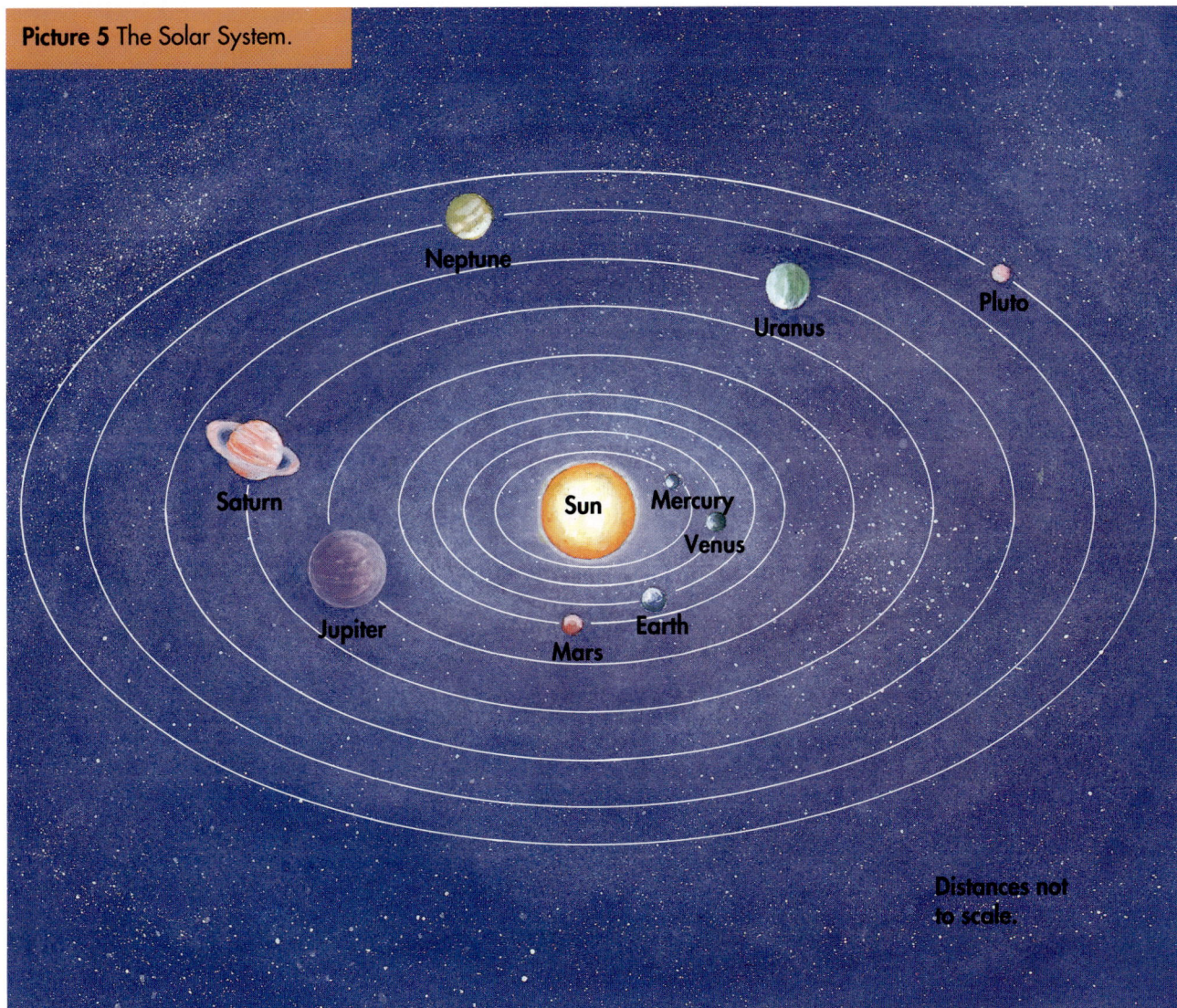

Picture 5 The Solar System.

Neptune
Pluto
Uranus
Saturn
Sun
Mercury
Venus
Jupiter
Earth
Mars

Distances not to scale.

Picture 1 The Montgolfier brothers' first attempt at flying.

1.6 Lighter than air

The Montgolfier brothers, Joseph and Etienne, owned a papermaking factory at Annonay, near Lyons, in France. The brothers longed to fly. But they had to be content with parachute jumping from the factory roof (picture 1).

The brothers discovered that a bag filled with smoke would rise above a fire of straw and wool. They believed that they had discovered a new gas – they called it 'electric smoke'. On 5th June 1783 they flew a silk balloon, lined with paper, and filled with 'electric smoke' from a fire-box. It travelled 1.6 km in its ten-minute flight.

Picture 2 The Montgolfier free-flight balloon.

But two months later, Professor Jacques Charles of the Paris Academy, launched a hydrogen balloon. He found that paper bags filled with the light gas, hydrogen, would rise into the air. Etienne travelled to Paris to see the experiment. The race was on to be the first person to fly.

By September, the brothers had an 'electric smoke' balloon big enough to carry a man. Nobody knew what flying would do to a living creature, so to **test** their invention they sent a sheep, a duck and a cockerel on an eight-minute flight. They crashed into a tree and the sheep trod on the cockerel, but they all survived.

Meanwhile, Professor Charles was preparing his hydrogen balloon. The brothers had to move quickly. They wanted to fly themselves, but the King of France thought they were too important to be risked. He wanted to send up two condemned criminals.

But on 21st November, the intrepid Pilatre de Rozier, and his friend the Marquis d'Arlandes, made the first free flight in a Montgolfier balloon. They travelled 9 km in 25 minutes, until the fire-box that hung beneath the balloon burnt a hole in it. They descended slowly to the ground as the gas escaped. Souvenir hunters tore their jackets to pieces.

1 To what did the Montgolfier brothers give the name 'electric smoke'?

2 What really made the Montgolfiers' balloon go up?

3 Why would it have helped the brothers if they had really understood 'electric smoke'?

4 Why should scientists be careful not to rush their experiments like the balloon-makers?

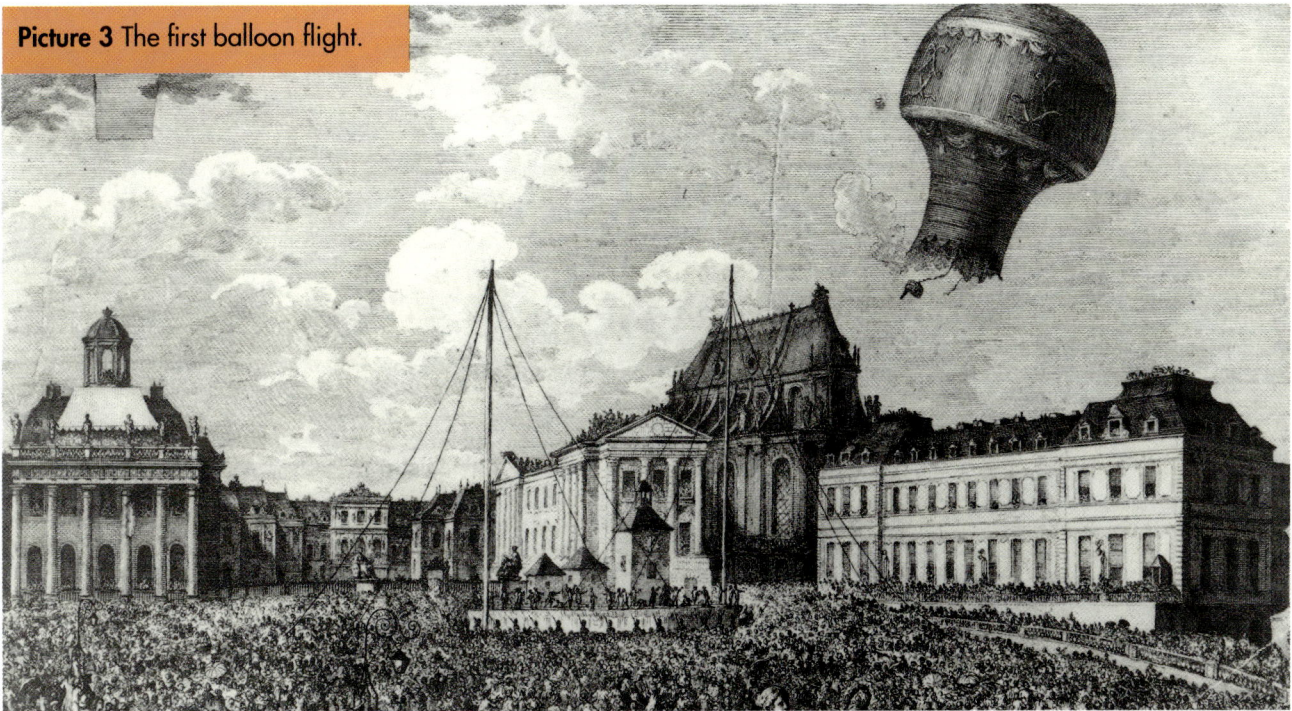
Picture 3 The first balloon flight.

A fortnight later, on 1st December, Professor Charles flew 43 km in his hydrogen balloon. He proved that a hydrogen balloon was easier to control than one with the Montgolfier's 'electric smoke'.

There were many more hydrogen balloon flights. Then in 1785, 'electric smoke' was proved to be only hot air.

Picture 4 Professor Charles's hydrogen balloon.

1.7 Is this science?

Telepathy

Some people claim a remarkable skill. They say that they can read people's minds and then tell what you are thinking. This is called *telepathy*.

You can test for this skill yourself. One traditional way uses a set of cards with geometrical shapes drawn on them. The first person shuffles the set of cards. Then they look at them, one at a time, thinking hard about the shapes.

The second person, the 'thought reader', says which shape the first person is thinking about.

Try it. Does it work? Always?

You might discover that you have 'thought reading' powers. But what are the chances of guessing the cards by luck alone? Try it. An activity like this is called a **control**. It can tell you a lot about your experimental results!

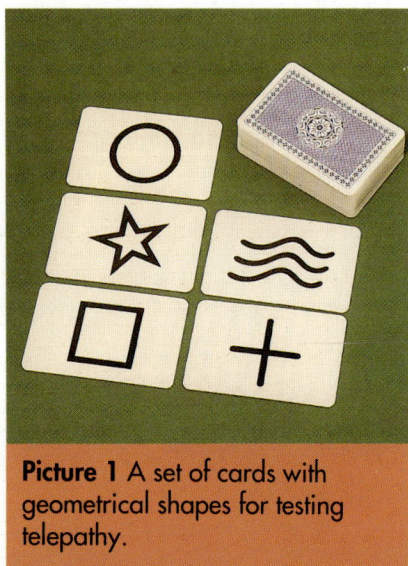

Picture 1 A set of cards with geometrical shapes for testing telepathy.

Telekinesis

Some people claim that they can move, or shape, things by the power of their minds. This is called *telekinesis*. One magician amazed people by his power in bending forks and spoons. Spoons and forks apparently bent in the kitchens of people watching him on television. But they also sometimes bent during recorded repeats of the programmes.

How would you test a person who claimed they could move things by telekinesis?

You would have to control some **variables**. What would they be?

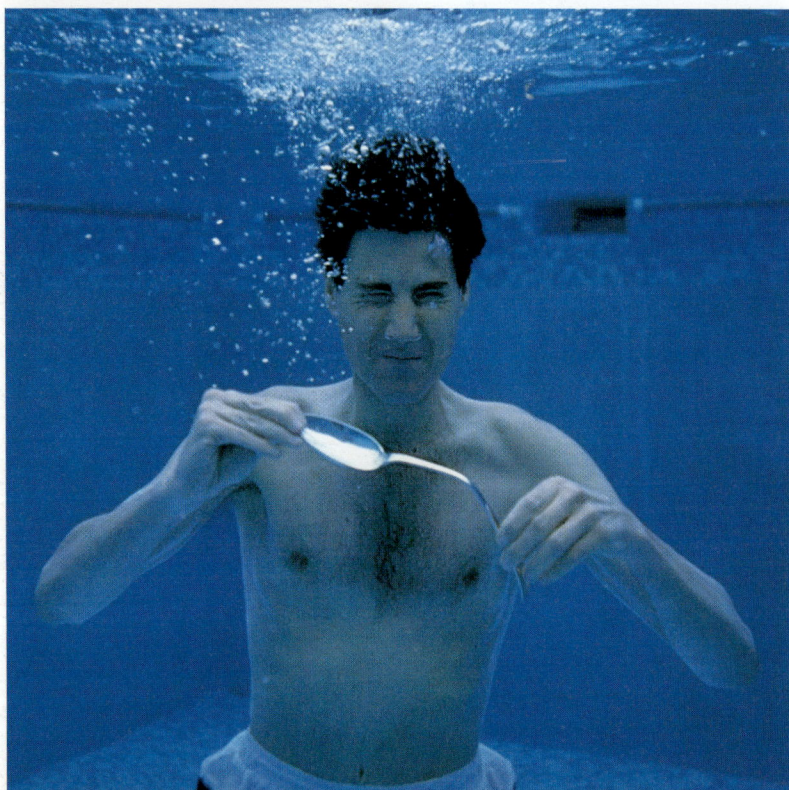

Picture 2 Uri Geller bending a spoon underwater.

Dowsing

Some people believe that a hazel twig can help you to find underground water. The twig should be Y-shaped and you are supposed to hold the two ends loosely in your hands and walk along (picture 3). When you cross underground water, the pointed end of the stick should twitch.

In fact, you can try dowsing with a coat hanger! Cut up a wire coat hanger to make two L-shaped pieces and hold the short ends loosely in your hands. Walk with the long ends pointing forward (picture 4). When you are over water (or metal) the wires may cross. Its that easy, but not always that reliable!

Science is **repeatable**. If a science experiment is a good one, it can be repeated, by you or other people, in the same conditions, to give the same results.

Scientists believe that the World is orderly and that the underlying laws remain the same even though the World may change. If someone said they could read minds, bend spoons, or find water, scientists would want to test that person under controlled conditions.

QUESTIONS

1 How could you test dowsing wires as water detectors?

2 What would you use as a control?

3 What are the variables when you walk across some gravel carrying two bent pieces of wire?

4 Dowsing doesn't always work. Can it be called science? Why?

5 What do you think makes the dowsing wires cross? Discuss some ideas with friends. Your guess is what scientists call a hypothesis.

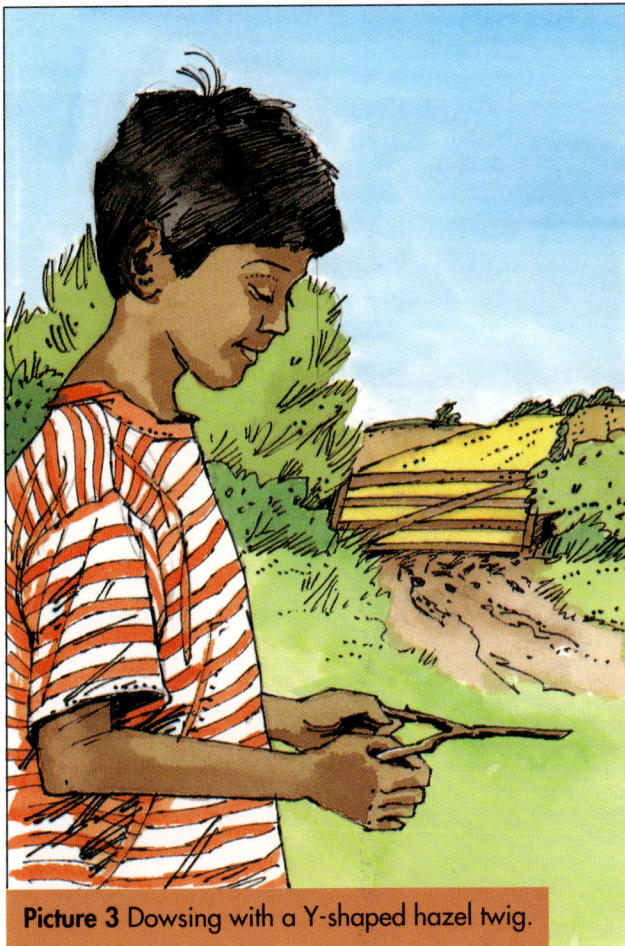

Picture 3 Dowsing with a Y-shaped hazel twig.

Picture 4 Dowsing with two L-shaped metal wires.

1.8 This is science!

James Clerk Maxwell (picture 1) studied the way that light waves travel. In 1864, he published his **hypothesis** – his theory. Nearly twenty-five years later, Heinrich Hertz (picture 2) discovered radio waves. They were very like light waves. Hertz knew that Maxwell's theory predicted that radio waves would behave like light waves.

Hertz was sure that he was right. He set up an **experiment** to prove the prediction. He **controlled** what he thought were important **variables**. But some things didn't seem important – the weather, the colour of the laboratory walls, the day of the week, the size of the laboratory. He ignored these.

Hertz found that radio and light waves travelled at different speeds. This was the opposite of his prediction from Maxwell's theory. Hertz died young – at the age of 37. After his death other people checked his figures. They found that they were wrong.

Hertz's experiment had been a poor one because waves had bounced off the laboratory walls, interfering with the measurements. The size of the laboratory had been very important, after all.

Picture 1 James Clerk Maxwell.

Picture 2 Heinrich Hertz.

Picture 3 Clerk Maxwell used this piece of apparatus in one of his experiments.

Scientific methods

Scientists like Hertz and Maxwell use scientific skills when they test a hypothesis. You use the same skills in your school science.

You **predict**. Hertz and Maxwell predicted that radio waves would go at the same speed as light waves.

You **plan** and design an experiment.

You **observe** and **measure**. Hertz observed that light and radio waves travelled at different speeds.

You **interpret** and **infer**. To infer is to draw conclusions. Hertz inferred that Maxwell's theory was wrong. You **evaluate** in order to assess or determine that a theory is correct. This was left to other scientists, after Hertz was dead. They found that his experiment was not a good one. He had not allowed for the size of the laboratory.

Hertz had not controlled all the possible variables. You must recognise and control all the possible variables, if you are going to design a fair test.

Your friend says that taller people are better arm-wrestlers than shorter people. When you ask why, your friend says that a tall fifteen-year-old has just beaten a short eleven-year-old three times out of three.

1 Why is this test unfair?

2 What variables has your friend ignored?

3 You observe that taller people do seem to win most often in arm-wrestling. Your hypothesis is that this has to do with their longer arms. How would you test this hypothesis, fairly?

Picture 4 Which variable did Hertz fail to control?

What happens next?

Science helps us to make predictions

Here are some short stories. They start, but they don't end. It's up to you to provide the end. Do it by discussing the stories in a group. Do as many as you can in the time you are given.

1 Simon hung a thin stick from a string. He blew up two identical balloons, and tied them to the ends of the stick. He balanced the balloons exactly – then he popped one. When the stick had stopped swinging …

What did the balance look like?
Why?

2 'My key's gone down the drain!' said Sophie.
'Never mind', said her big sister. 'I can see it, under the water. We'll get it with my magnet!'
'But magnets don't work under water' said Sophie.

Do they?
How could you find out?

3 'If I drop two identical objects of different masses from the top of a tower' said Galileo, 'they will hit the ground together'.
'Nonsense' said another scientist. 'The heavy one will hit the ground first'.

Galileo never tried the experiment.

Was he right or wrong?
How could you find out?

4 'The Earth is spinning all the time' said Max's Geography teacher. 'So if I throw a ball straight up', said Max, 'it can never come down just where I am!'

Was Max right?
Why?

5 'Everything falls towards the middle of the Earth' said Rachel. 'So if I dropped a ball when I was standing on the Moon it would fly off into space, and back to Earth'.
'Of course it wouldn't', said Sue. 'But it would do funny things!'

Who was right?
How and why?

6 'Giraffes have stretched up into trees to eat leaves for millions of years' said Hardip's brother. 'That's why their necks have got longer and longer.'
'That's right,' said Hardip. 'And if people go on travelling in cars, we'll soon have no legs left'.

Were they right?
How and why?

2.1 What's it like out there?

A changing World

The World we live in is a changing place. That's obvious if you get caught on the beach by a high tide or sudden storm.

Many disasters are caused by natural changes – like drought or flood, landslide or volcano. We need to know if changes are about to happen to our climate, or to the Earth's crust itself.

What do you think the people living in San Francisco City (picture 2) have done to protect themselves, since the earthquake there in 1989?

Picture 1 Waiting for the rain to finish and tennis to begin.

Picture 2 An earthquake is a major change in the Earth's crust.

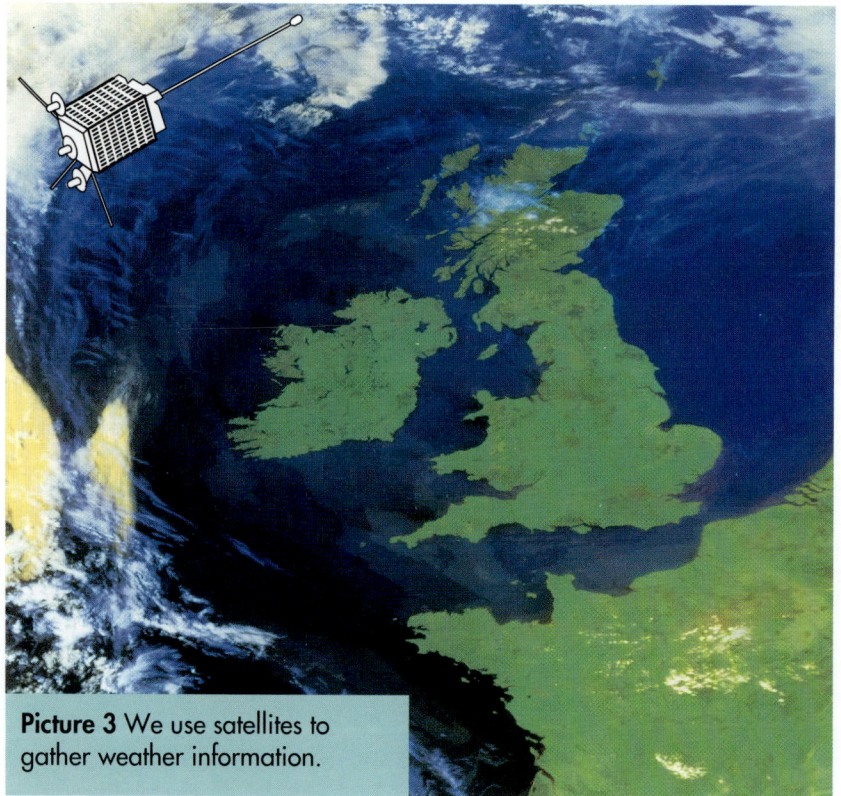

Picture 3 We use satellites to gather weather information.

Scientists collect and study a lot of weather information, so they can understand weather patterns. From these patterns they can predict or **forecast** what will happen in the future. Weather forecasts are useful because we can get ready for sudden weather changes, like snow or hurricanes. A weather forecast may be a warning to sailors of trouble ahead. Farmers time planting and harvesting according to the weather.

What changes?

Weather changes affect living things. To **survive** living things must **respond**. Earthworms can't swim or breathe under water, so if their burrows fill up with water during a heavy rainstorm they're in trouble. They respond by leaving the burrow and coming out onto the surface.

Nature detectives

We can see signs of change by looking for nature's clues. Leaf fall and bird migration are both signs of the winter approaching. Some people believe that cows lie down when it's about to rain. How would you find out if this is really true?

Table 1 Weather data for Dale Fort and Ringway.

MONTH	Temperature extremes (°C) (over one month)		Rainfall (mm) (average daily total)	Sunshine (hours) (average daily total)
	Maximum	Minimum		
January 1990	11.9	1.9	4.0	1.9
	13.7	−0.9	3.8	2.0
June 1990	18.0	9.9	2.5	6.1
	22.6	5.5	2.8	3.6
October 1990	18.4	7.3	3.3	3.3
	20.8	1.4	3.6	2.6

Dale Fort (Dyfed, Wales)

Ringway (Greater Manchester, England)

The data shown in table 1 was collected by the Meteorological Office. Which place you would prefer to live in if you had a choice?

Picture 5

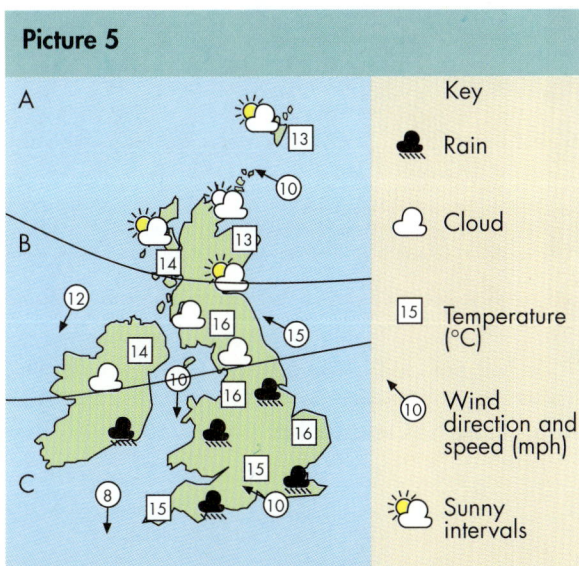

Key

🐾 Rain

☁ Cloud

15 Temperature (°C)

↖10 Wind direction and speed (mph)

🌤 Sunny intervals

1 A seismograph detects movement in the Earth's crust. What changes can it warn us about?

2 What change do you think the daisies in picture 4 are responding to?

Picture 4 The petals of Livingstone daisies open wide in warm sunshine and close when clouds pass over.

3 Picture 5 is a weather map for 13 October 1992. The key explains what the symbols mean. Lines are used to indicate three areas on the map: *A* Northern Scotland; *B* Southern Scotland, Northern Ireland and the North of England; *C* Southern Ireland, The Midlands, Wales and the South of England.
(a) Describe what the weather was like on 13 October 1992 in areas *A*, *B* and *C*.
(b) Which area had
(i) the strongest wind?
(ii) the highest temperatures?

4 (a) Display the data in table 1 in the form of a barchart.
(b) What are the main differences in the weather at Dale Fort and Ringway?

5 Jane Shaw wants to set up a business growing tomatoes in greenhouses.
What weather information would help her decide where to set up the business in the UK?

2.2 Survival

Why is survival important?

The instinct to survive is very strong. When placed in water, even newborn babies try to swim 'doggy paddle'. They don't have to learn how to do it, it's an **instinct** or inherited skill.

The survival instinct means that each individual has the urge to live. The longer things live, the more likely they are to become adults. So there's more chance of them **reproducing**. So the survival instinct is a way of making sure of new generations in the future.

Being well adapted

All living things inherit their **characteristics** from their parents. Over very many generations, characteristics may evolve that help them survive. They may become **well adapted** to their surroundings or **environment**. This means that different types of living things become adapted to live in different places.

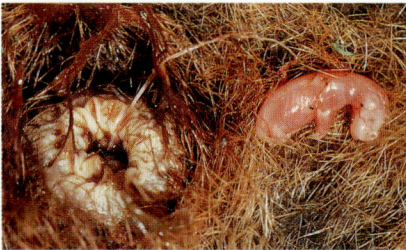

Picture 1 What a journey for a Joey! It's an instinct that makes a newborn baby kangaroo travel about 15 cm to find its food – mum's milk.

Picture 2 The orchid's roots hang out into the moist air and absorb water.

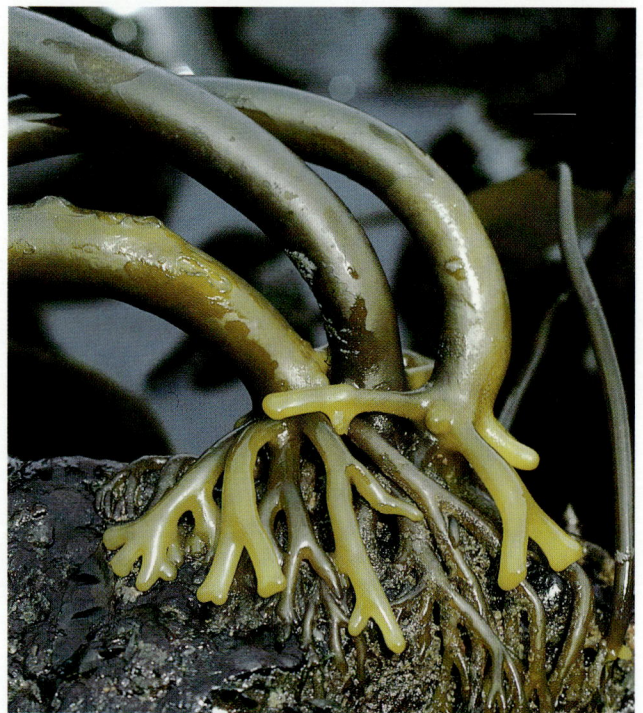

Picture 3 Hold on! Seaweeds are often battered by fierce waves. But they survive because their shape is well adapted.

Each organism may be successful in its own surroundings or **habitat**, but may not survive in another. The orchid in picture 2 is adapted for life in the rain forests of Brazil. It's found high up on the branches of large trees.

Animals can be well adapted to their environment too. Much of a baby seal's body is fat – fat that is vital for keeping its body warm. African elephants have big ears that lose heat, helping the elephant to cool down. Earthworms are slimy, so they don't dry up.

Danger!

Keeping out of trouble is a serious business for most animals. You may think that a zebra's stripes make them easy to see. But looking for one zebra in a herd is confusing. It's an example of **camouflage** – a way of blending in with the background. A snail has its own armour to protect it from attack and injury.

Picture 4 Where is it? A stick insect is well camouflaged.

Frogs are slimy to touch. If you've tried holding them you'll know how slippery they feel. The slime tastes nasty too, so they're less likely to be eaten by enemies.

Often a **quick reaction** is what's needed to keep out of danger. A hedgehog rolls up into a prickly ball that isn't easy to eat. Squids squirt ink and swim away before their enemies can catch them.

But other **ways of behaving** are important too. Many animals hide, in burrows underground, or build nests at the tops of trees.

1 Why is the 'survival instinct' important to the human population?

2 Mammals all have some sort of hair, or fur, or wool. How does this help them survive?

3 Draw up a table of examples of features that help living things survive. Use these headings:

Living thing	Survival feature	How it helps the living thing survive

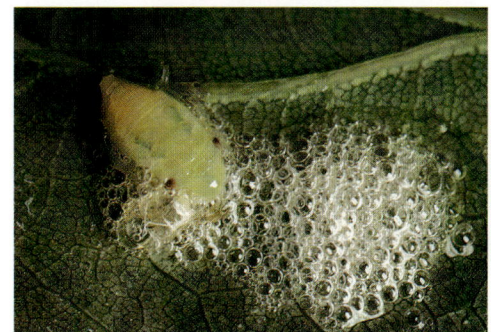

Picture 5 Hidden in spit … a spittle bug pumps a soapy liquid out of its body, and froths it up with air bubbles.

Picture 1 Amazonian tribes live in forest homes.

2.3 A good place to live?

The locality you live in means the area nearby. Many different types of living things may be found there. Each has its own **habitat** or place to live.

Living things need **space** to live and breed. They gain a **supporting surface** – somewhere to rest. Many animals build a shelter to protect themselves from changes in climate, or from enemies. The habitat must offer **food** too. If resources are limited, living things have to **compete** with each other. Gannets compete for space to nest on rocky cliff ledges. If there isn't enough space, then some birds won't be able to breed.

Picture 2 Not everyone has a home.

Picture 3 The crab is a messy eater. The food particles it drops are eaten by the anemones living on its shell.

Life on the outside and on the inside

Just about everywhere you can think of, is home for something. Even living things themselves make good places to live. The hermit crab in picture 3 has a sea anemone on the **outside** of its shell. The anemone's stinging tentacles keep enemies away.

Some things find homes on the **inside**, like the microbes in your intestines. They use part of the food you eat but in return, some help us to digest vegetables, or make vitamins we need.

Looking for signs

Many animals are shy of people, and aren't easy to find. They may be active at night, when darkness hides them from enemies. Animal signs like paw prints, burrows, nests of webs, tufts of fur and the remains of food like half-eaten nuts are all good clues.

Picture 4 A fox's droppings are very distinctive. They're sausage-shaped with a twisted point at one end. The colour depends on what the fox has eaten.

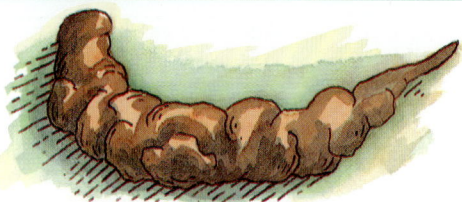

Can a study be accurate?

Have you ever wondered how many blades of grass there are? To be totally accurate you'd have to count them all – an almost impossible job. But you could **sample** a small part of the locality you're studying. Then you could **estimate** how many there might be in the whole area.

Picture 5 This quadrat is being used to count the number of different plants in 1 m² of a field.

Metal frame or string, pegged down at the corners

A **quadrat** is frame you can use to sample a small area. You throw the quadrat over your shoulder and then you count the number of organisms inside. You can mark out a line called a **transect** and record the living things growing along the line.

Scientists take as many samples as they can. This gives them more information to study. Usually it's necessary to use mathematics to help understand the information. Finding averages is one simple way of doing this.

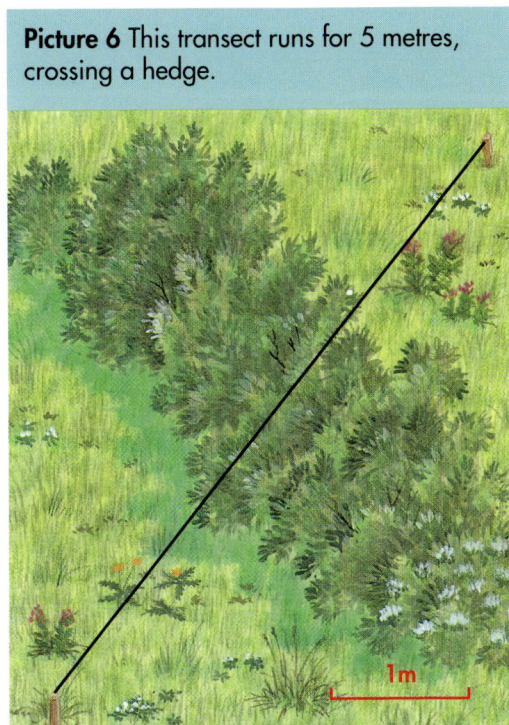

Picture 6 This transect runs for 5 metres, crossing a hedge.

1 m

1 (a) Make a list of all the signs of animals that you might find in a woodland.
 (b) What does a woodland offer to the plants and animals living there?

2 A square quadrat with sides 1 m long was used to take five samples of plants in chalky grassland. The results are shown below in picture 7.

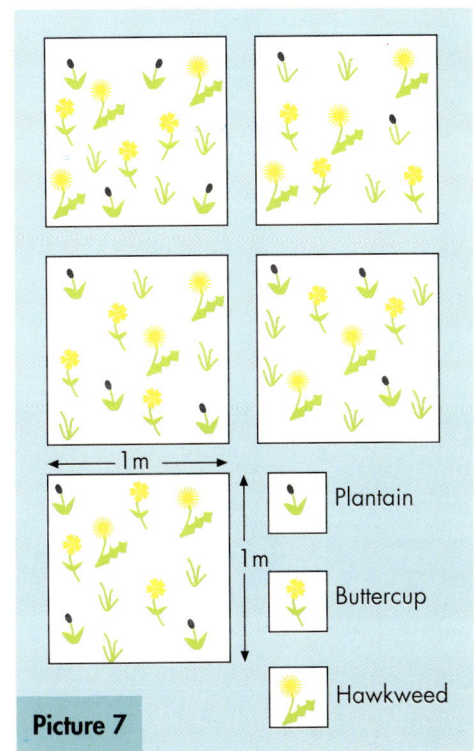

1 m

Plantain

1 m

Buttercup

Hawkweed

Picture 7

The number of grass plants was not counted.
Find the average number per metre² of plantain, buttercup and hawkweed plants.

3 Use books to help you find out which living things might be found in these habitats: *a compost heap; hedgerow; a rock pool; a dog's intestines; a garden pond.*

Picture 1 A key for sorting imaginary spiders.

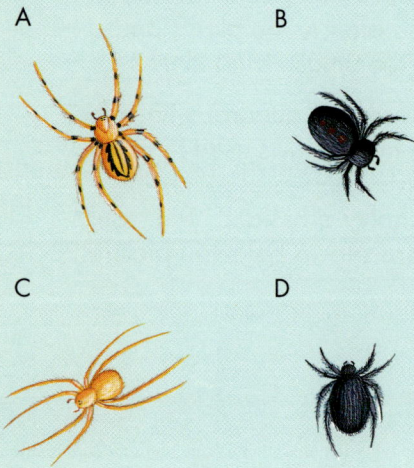

2.4 Sort it out

Sorting by feature

Scientists find it useful to **sort** information. Living things are sorted into groups according to the **differences** between them. Each group then contains living things with similar features.

You could use one difference to sort humans, like their sex. This gives two groups, males and females. If you add a second difference like curly or straight hair, you would end up with four groups. Then the people in each group would be similar in two ways – sex and hair type. The more differences you use, the more similar the people are within each group.

Using a key

A **key** is a chart that helps you sort things by feature. Here's an example of a key for sorting spiders – imaginary ones, with made-up names! Look at one of the five spiders which are drawn above the key. Start at the top and work down through the features. Use the pictures to find which spider is which.

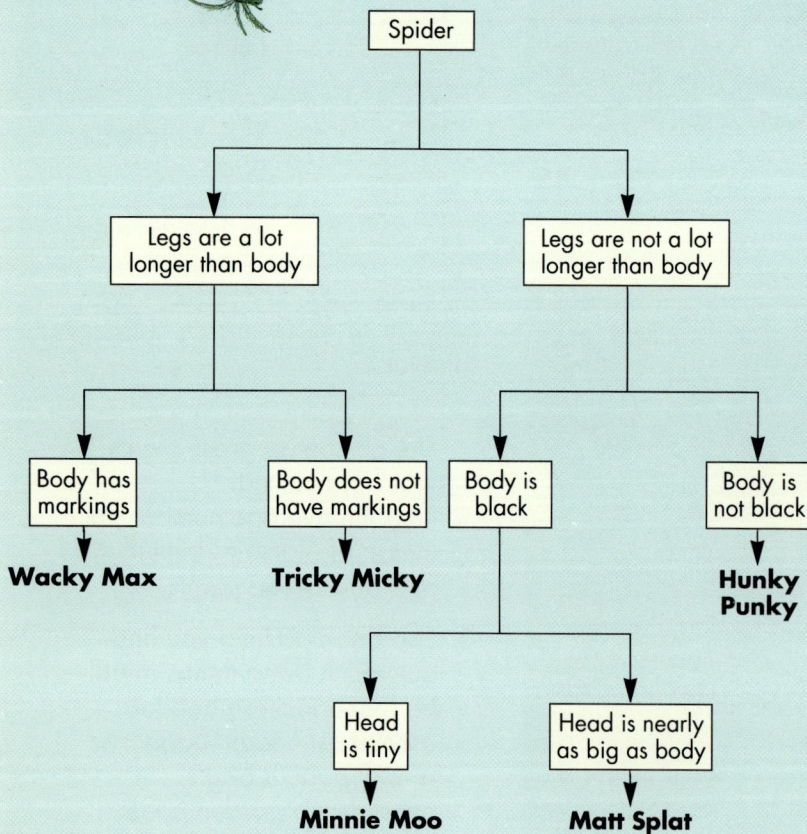

Tree puzzle

Oak, ash, elm, beech and horse chestnut are some common tree types which grow in the UK. You may recognise some of these trees. But could you identify them from a single leaf?

Use the key in picture 2 to find out which leaf comes from each tree. Follow the instructions and you should come to the name of each tree. This is a very simple key, so other leaves might fit these descriptions. To identify other types of leaves, other differences would be used.

Picture 2 Solving a tree puzzle.

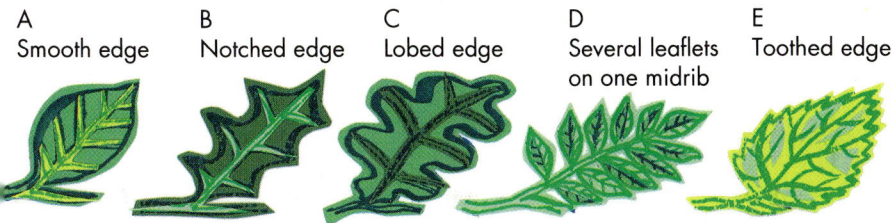

A
Smooth edge

B
Notched edge

C
Lobed edge

D
Several leaflets
on one midrib

E
Toothed edge

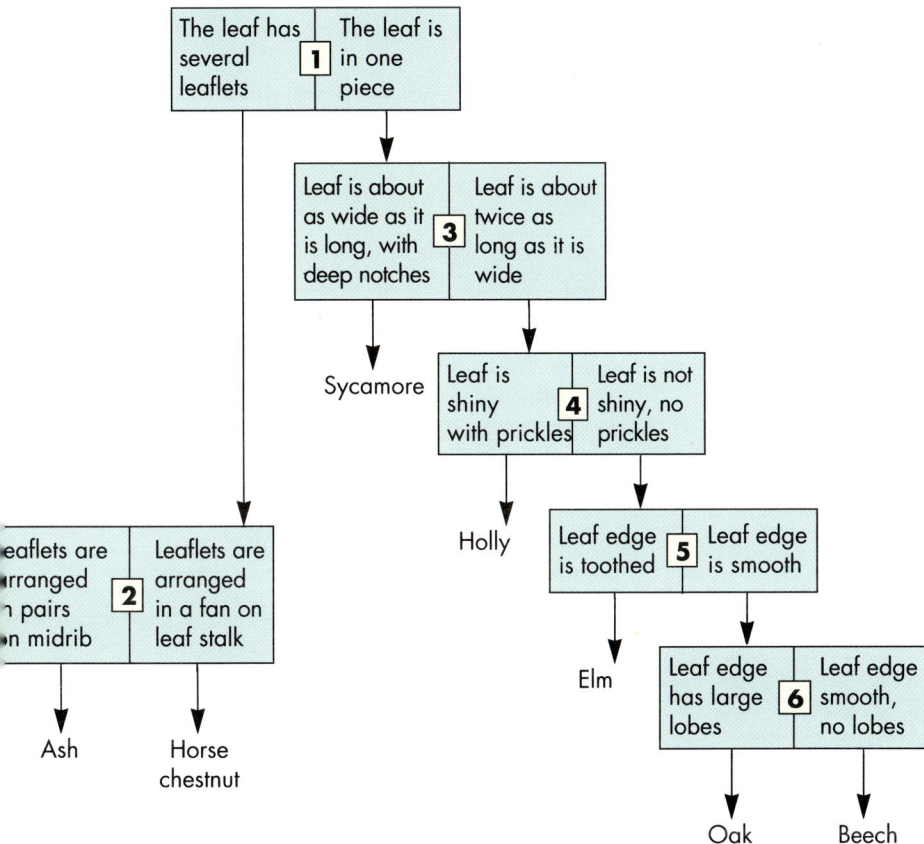

The leaf has several leaflets	**1**	The leaf is in one piece

Leaf is about as wide as it is long, with deep notches	**3**	Leaf is about twice as long as it is wide

Sycamore

Leaf is shiny with prickles	**4**	Leaf is not shiny, no prickles

Holly

Leaf edge is toothed	**5**	Leaf edge is smooth

Elm

Leaf edge has large lobes	**6**	Leaf edge smooth, no lobes

Oak   Beech

eaflets are rranged n pairs n midrib	**2**	Leaflets are arranged in a fan on leaf stalk

Ash

Horse chestnut

More advanced sorting

If someone loses blood during an accident or operation, they may be given blood from another person – a **blood transfusion**. Before this century blood transfusions weren't successful. Then in 1900, Karl Landsteiner discovered that peoples' blood showed chemical differences, which were used to sort blood into different **blood groups**. Now patients always receive blood of their own blood group, and transfusions are successful.

Picture 3 Blood Transfusion Service Logo.

QUESTIONS

1 Use the key to identify the creature in picture 4.

Picture 4

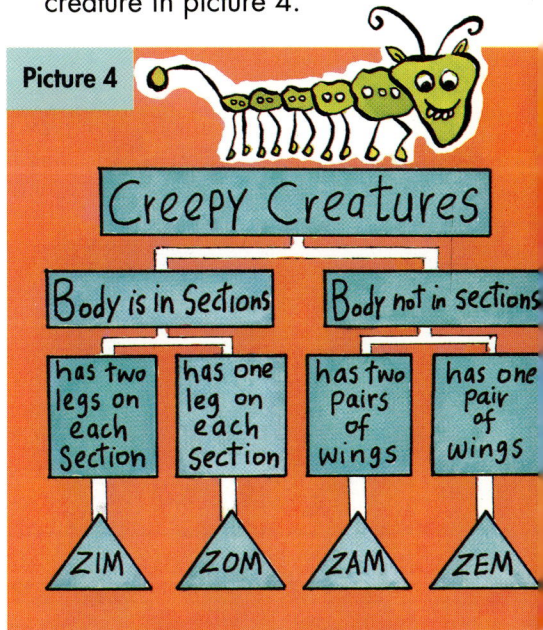

2 Picture 5 shows ten drawings of 'Liquorice All-Sorts'. Work out a key for sorting them into four different groups.

Picture 5

Compare your key with other students' keys. Did you all use the same ideas?

3 Toys for young children often involve sorting blocks according to shape. How would you sort the shapes in picture 6 into groups?

Picture 6

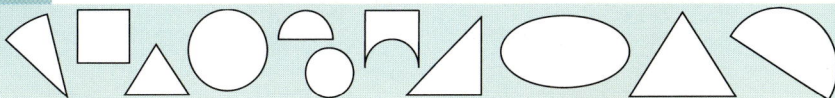

2.5 Classification of living things

Kingdoms

Putting living things into groups is called **classification**. Table 1 gives you some idea of the huge variety of different living things.

Table 1 Living things in five big groups – the kingdoms.

Kingdom	Features
Bacteria	**Bacteria** are microscopic. Some cause disease. Most are harmless and sometimes useful, like those involved in making cheese and yoghurt and those that help dead animals and plants to decay.
Protoctists	Many **protoctists** are tiny like diatoms, while others like seaweeds are larger. They all live in watery habitats.
Fungi	Yeasts and moulds are types of **fungi**. Moulds have thread-like bodies which produce spores, sometimes within a spore body called a mushroom.
Plants	**Plants** are green because they contain chlorophyll. They can make their own food.
Animals	**Animals** feed on other living things. They usually move about.

Picture 1 A giraffe with a fly on its nose.

Animal groups

Both the giraffe and fly in picture 1 belong to the animal kingdom, and yet they are very different. So kingdoms are split up into smaller groups too. For animals, the first important question to ask, is 'Does it have a backbone?' Animals without a backbone are called **invertebrates**. You can find out more about them in topic 2.6.

Table 2 The famous five – five groups of vertebrates.

Vertebrate group	Features
Fish	**Fish** live and breed in water. Their skins are scaly and they breathe through gills.
Amphibians	Frogs, newts and toads are types of **amphibians**. They need to live near water, so they can keep their skins wet and lay their eggs.
Reptiles	The **reptile** group includes snakes, lizards and crocodiles. Their skins are dry and they lay eggs with shells.
Birds	Beaks and feathers belong to **birds**. Birds' eggs also have shells to protect them from damage and drying out.
Mammals	**Mammals** are hairy. The females can make milk to suckle their young.

Back to backbones

Animals with a backbone are called **vertebrates**. Each vertebrate group has its own special features. Table 2 shows the five groups.

Body temperature

Even on a cold winter's day your body temperature is about 37°C. It only changes slightly if you're ill. Your body has ways of keeping its temperature constant. But an ant or snake can't do this. Their bodies get warmer or colder according to the weather. Only birds and mammals have constant body temperature.

QUESTIONS

1 Draw four boxes in a row, and link them with arrows to make a flowchart.

   Arrange the words in the list below in order of size. Start with the word for largest groups in the left-hand box. *living thing; orang-utan; kingdom; vertebrate*

2 It isn't always easy to tell whether an animal has a backbone. Why not?

3 Give an example of
   (*a*) a mammal that lives in the sea.
   (*b*) a flying mammal.
   (*c*) a mammal that lives underground.
   (*d*) a tree-living mammal.

2.6 Living without a backbone

Animals without a backbone are called **invertebrates**. They're usually small because they have no bones to support their bodies.

Worms use liquid pressure to keep their bodies firm, rather like a hot water bottle when it's very full. Insects have a hard protective outer coat. It supports them and their muscles are attached to it.

The invertebrate group is very large, so it's divided into smaller groups.

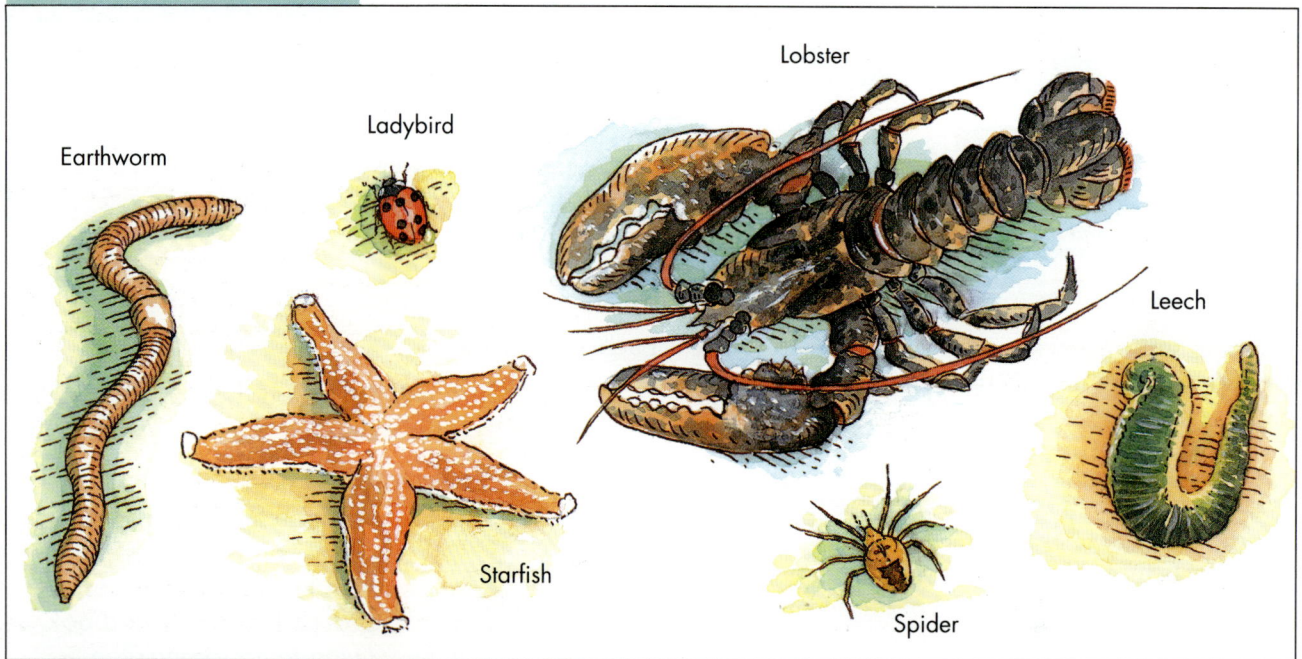

Picture 1 Spineless wonders!

Earthworm

Ladybird

Lobster

Leech

Starfish

Spider

Picture 2 Snails are molluscs.

Worms are important invertebrates. There are many types of worms, but earthworms are the ones we know best. There are millions of them in the soil. By eating dead bits of plants, earthworms help to clear away nature's rubbish. The waste they make fertilises the soil. Other sorts of worms can live in animals' guts, using the food they find there. A tapeworm is an example.

Molluscs are invertebrates with soft bodies. They sometimes have shells. Some live on land like the snail shown in picture 2. The biggest mollusc is the giant squid. Weighing in at several tonnes, it grows up to 16 metres in length!

Arthropods – the biggest group of invertebrates

There are many different kinds of **arthropods**. They all have some similar features:

- their bodies have a **hard covering – the exoskeleton**
- they're built in a pattern of **segments**
- the legs and feelers have **joints**.

The arthropod group is divided into four different subgroups. Each subgroup is slightly different, although they all have the three arthropod features described above.

Picture 3 Arthropods with a difference.

Look at each animal in picture 4. Decide if they are arthropods. If they are, what subgroup should each belong to?

Picture 4 Some invertebrates.

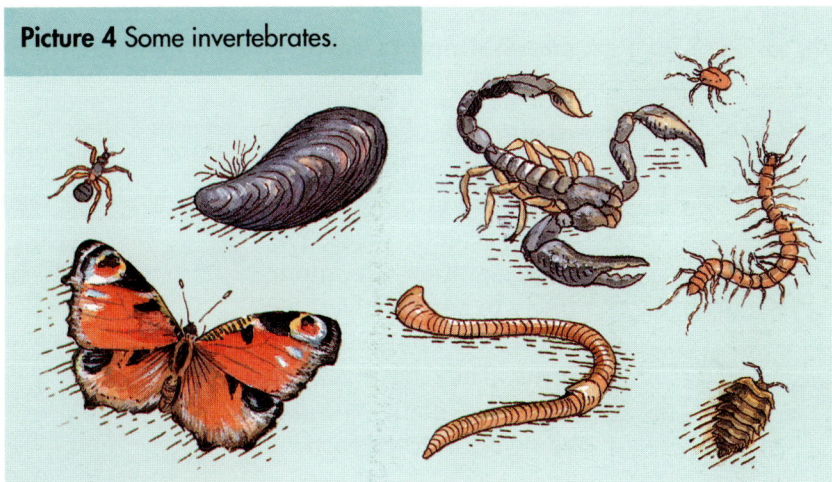

1 What is
(a) an invertebrate?
(b) an arthropod?

2 Imagine collecting some leafy soil from a wood. What invertebrates might you find in the soil sample?

3 Both of the animals in picture 5 are invertebrates, but only one is an arthropod.

Picture 5

Roundworm   Housefly

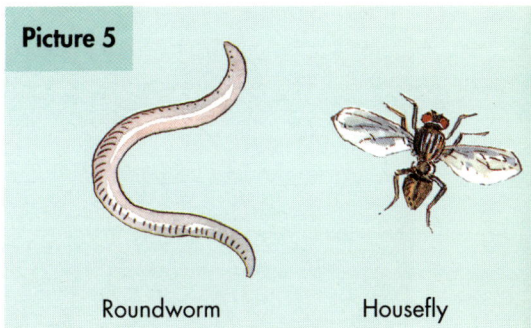

Say which one the arthropod is, and explain how you made the choice.

4 (a) Describe some of the ways that invertebrates support and protect their bodies.
(b) Why are most invertebrates small in size?
(c) Give an example of one invertebrate which is not small, and explain how its body is supported.

31

2.7 The green kingdom

Picture 1 Green as far as the eye can see …

Plants feed the World. They use green **chlorophyll** to absorb some of the Sun's energy. Energy is needed by the plant leaves to make food. It's a process that feeds the whole World, since animals can't make their own food.

Which plants make spores?

Plants like **mosses** have very simple bodies without real roots. They live in damp places and absorb water all over their surface.

A **fern** stands taller than a moss, so that much of its body is in the air (see picture 2). It can live in drier places and has simple roots that collect water from the soil. Both mosses and ferns make tiny **spores** during their life cycles. New plants grow from these spores. Once, forests of tree ferns covered the earth, and coal formed from them when they died.

Which plants make seeds?

Plants like flowers, shrubs and trees are more complicated than simple mosses and ferns. Water can easily move up their roots, through their stems and to their leaves because they have special transport systems. They have strong support systems to hold them up.

Conifers and **flowering plants** make seeds. Seeds are a successful way of reproducing new plants. Seeds have a protective coat, so they are more likely to survive than the spores of mosses and ferns. They have a tiny embryo plant inside, along with stored food.

Picture 2 Fantastic forests of tree ferns grow in New Zealand. They give us clues about ancient tree fern forests.

Picture 3 These two coconut seeds are sprouting.

Conifers

Plants that have **cones** are called **conifers**. Their seeds lie between the woody scales of the cone.

Picture 4 Christmas conifer.

Picture 5 Banana seeds are found inside these fruits.

Flowering plants

Flowering plants have flowers. They may be big like roses or small like daisies. After **pollination**, part of the flower becomes a **seed**. Seeds are found within a **fruit**. We're used to seeing seeds inside delicious fruits like peaches and apples. Other fruits are only a coat around the seed, like the winged fruit of a sycamore tree.

A green key

1 Why do all living things depend on plants?

2

Picture 7

A

B

C

D

Use the key to the plant kingdom in picture 6 to put plants A, B, C and D (in picture 7) into groups.

3 Seeds won't grow unless they are given the right conditions.

Describe how you would investigate the conditions that make seeds grow well.

Plant Kingdom

Plants with spores

Leaves and stems, but no real roots

Leaves and stem and simple roots

Mosses

Ferns

Plants with seeds

Seeds form in a cone

Seeds form in fruits

Flowering plants

Conifers

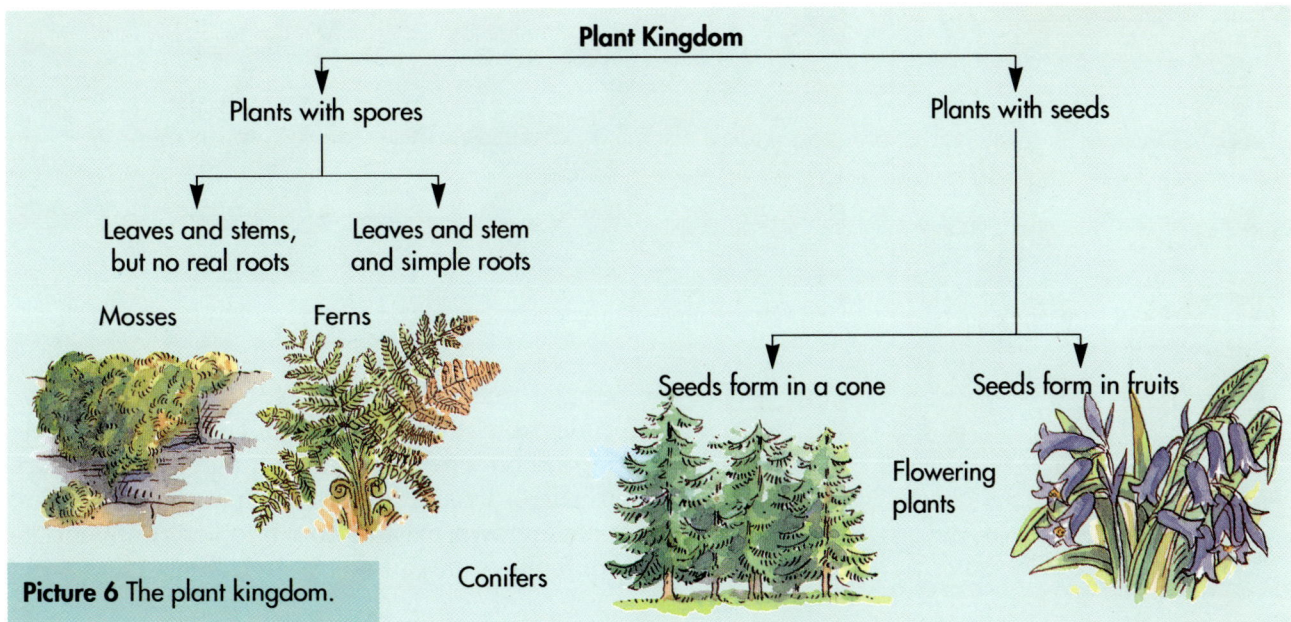

Picture 6 The plant kingdom.

2.8 Looking at variation

Picture 1 Similarities and differences.

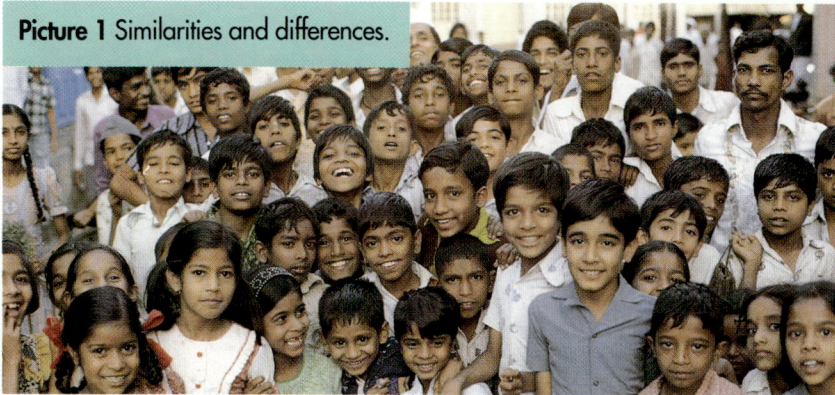

Similar – but not the same

All humans belong to the same species. If you check back to topic 2.5, you'll see we share some features with other mammals. Picture 1 shows that people can have similar features. However, there are many differences between people too. These differences are examples of **variation**.

Why are people different?

When a couple have children they pass on their features in a **genetic code**. These features are called **inherited characteristics**. They help decide how we develop, as you can see from family photographs.

Picture 3 a Claire and Jane – 6 years old. b Claire and Jane – 21 years old.

Picture 2 Family characteristics caught on film.

How people live can also make a difference. Identical twins receive the same genetic code from their parents, but can look slightly different. It might depend on what they ate, or if they enjoyed sport, or if they dyed their hair, or lived in different climates. The identical twins in picture 3b have grown up and now live very different life styles. These sort of differences are caused by **environmental factors**.

34

Measuring variation

Some of the differences between people are very obvious, like the one which is shown in picture 4. You can either roll your tongue, or you can't. Try it! You could investigate this type of difference by counting the people who can tongue roll and the people who can't.

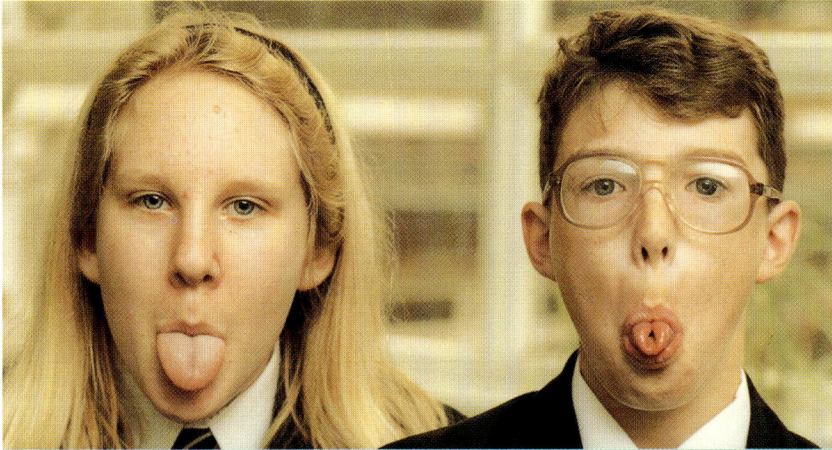

Picture 4 Can you, or can't you?

There are lots of other differences which we can measure, like height and mass. The information can be fed into a computer and analysed. This is how the Government put together number facts (statistics) about a population (see graph 1).

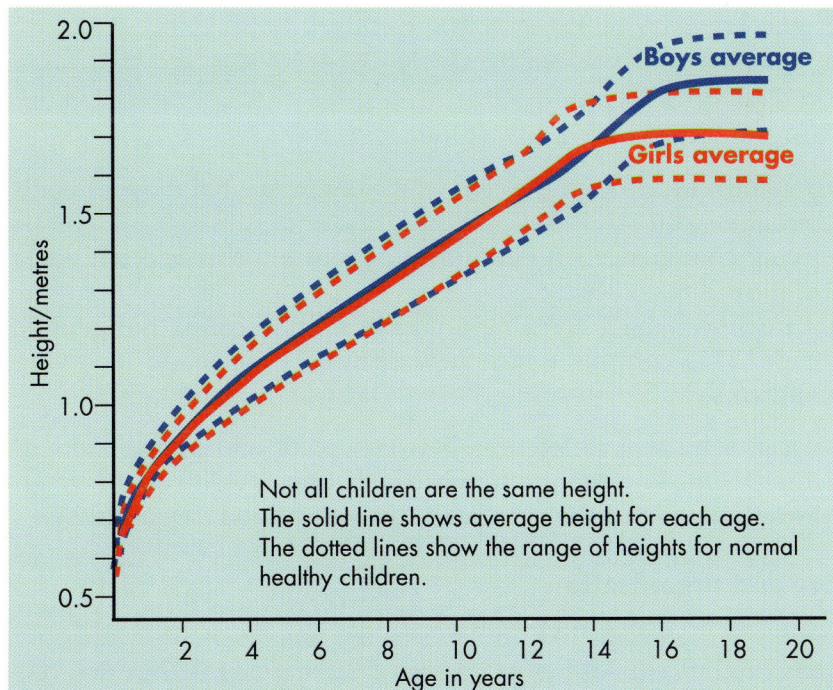

Not all children are the same height.
The solid line shows average height for each age.
The dotted lines show the range of heights for normal healthy children.

Graph 1 Variation in patterns of growth for children living in Britain.

1 What is meant by *variation*?

2 Look at the list of rose features shown below:
colour, size of flower, type of scent, height of bush, presence of thorns.

Which of these features do you think are decided by
(a) genetic code (inherited)?
(b) environmental factors?

3 How would you investigate the variation in foot size of people in your class?

4 Look at the growth charts in graph 1.
(a) What do you notice about the heights of boys and girls up to the age of 11?
(b) What range of heights is normal for
(i) boys aged 13?
(ii) girls aged 13?
(c) What is the height pattern for boys and girls after the age of 13?

35

2.9 Building blocks of life

How are living things organised?

Living things are built of units called **cells**, like a wall is made of bricks. A cell is the smallest unit of life. Although there are many different types of cell, they all have some similar features.

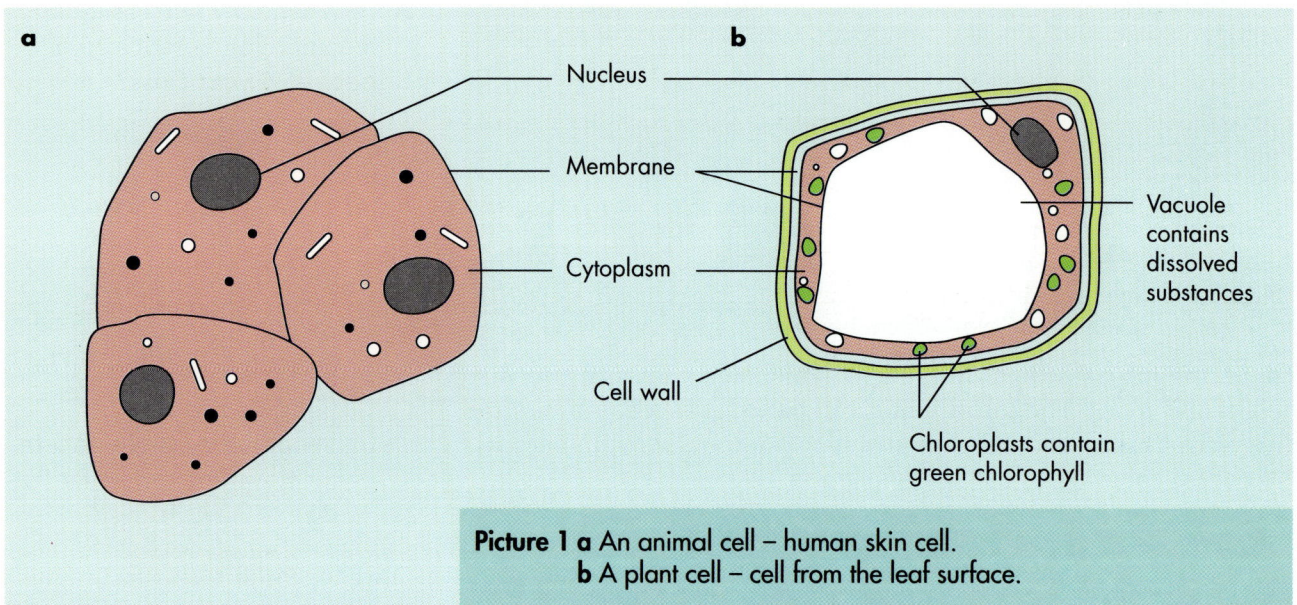

Picture 1 **a** An animal cell – human skin cell.
b A plant cell – cell from the leaf surface.

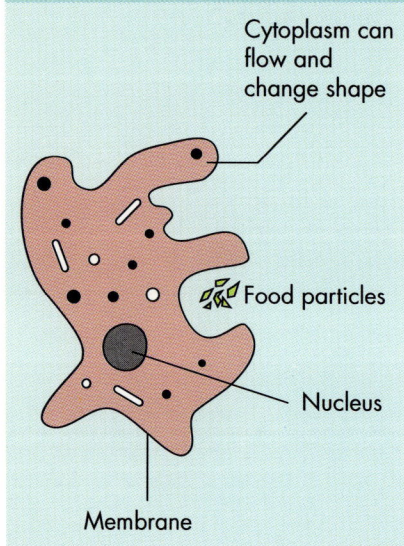

Picture 2 Life in one cell.

These are some key features of living cells:

- a **membrane** around the cell, which controls what moves in and out of the cell
- living contents called **cytoplasm**, where the chemical activities of the cell takes place
- a **nucleus** which contains a chemical code called the **genetic code**. This controls which new materials are made including new cells.

You can see some differences between plant and animal cells in picture 1. One important difference is that plant cells contain green **chlorophyll**, so that they can make their own food (see topic 2.7).

Size and organisation

Some tiny organisms like an Amoeba are *unicellular*. They are only made of one cell. All the processes of life happen within that one cell. Picture 2 shows the cytoplasm of an Amoeba cell flowing around food particles. Once surrounded, the food is digested.

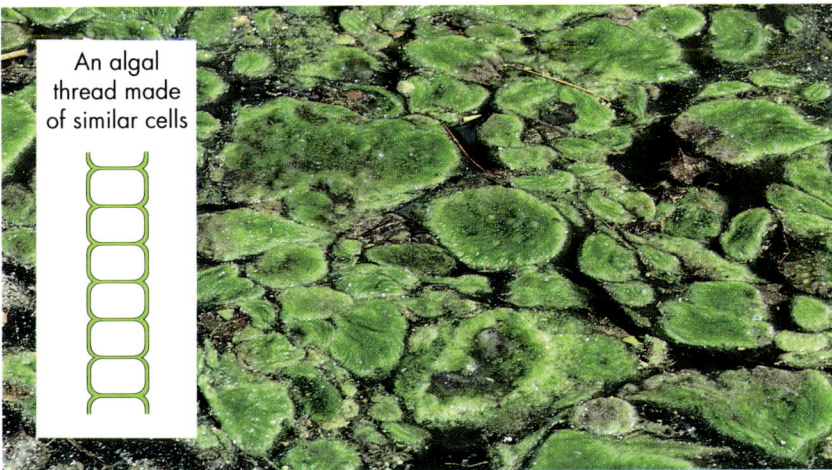

An algal thread made of similar cells

Picture 3 Algae can grow fast in summer, clogging up ponds and streams.

Bigger living things may be made of *groups* of similar cells, like the algae shown in picture 3. You can often see these threads forming mats near the surface of a pond in summer.

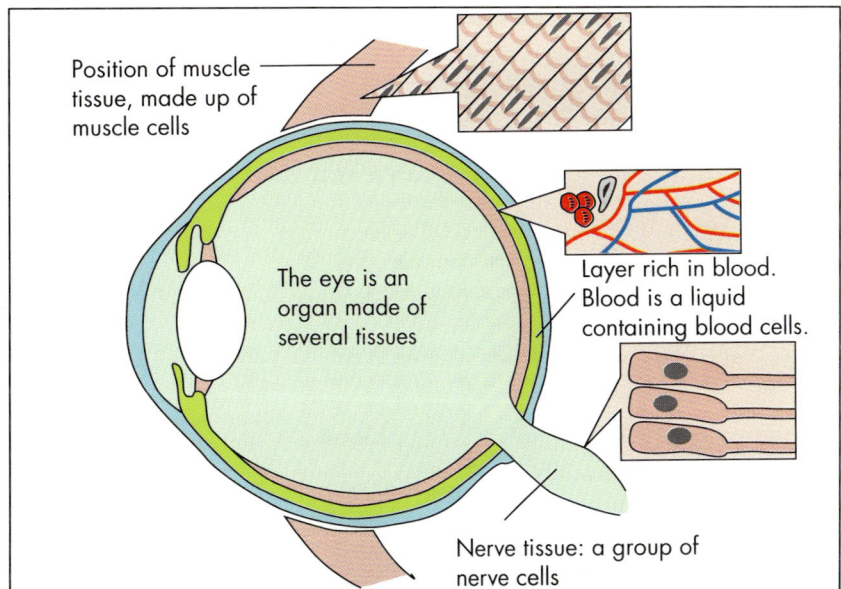

Picture 4 **a** Red blood cells **b** Muscle cells **c** Nerve cells

- A nerve **cell** in the eye has a special job to do. It detects light patterns entering the eye.
- The tails of lots of nerve cells collect into a bundle forming nerve **tissue**, which carries messages to the brain.
- The eye is an **organ**. It's made of several tissues like muscle, blood and nerve tissue.

Your body is a sophisticated machine built of cells, tissues and organs. How many of those organs can you name?

Building blocks of bodies

More complex living things like humans may have many different types of cells. Cells can be very different, depending on the job they do.

Picture 5 gives an example of how parts of the body are built up from cells, tissues and organs.

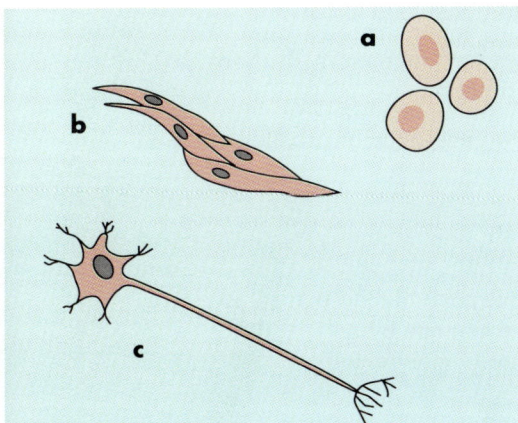

Position of muscle tissue, made up of muscle cells

The eye is an organ made of several tissues

Layer rich in blood. Blood is a liquid containing blood cells.

Nerve tissue: a group of nerve cells

Picture 5 Cells, tissues and organs.

QUESTIONS

1 Copy this table into your book. Fill in the blanks.

Part of cell	What it does
Cytoplasm	
Membrane	
Nucleus	

2 What are the main differences between plant and animal cells?

3 You may need to use resource books to help you answer this question. Name these parts of your body:
   (*a*) a tissue that stops you drying out.
   (*b*) an organ that allows gases to move in and out.
   (*c*) a tissue that supports you.
   (*d*) an organ that is made mostly of muscle.

Picture 1 Which is dead and which is alive?

2.10 Being alive

Dead and alive

A chair and a living tree are both made out of wood, but only one of them is alive. What is it about the tree which means it's living? A living thing carries out **life processes**, which stop when it dies. Box 1 describes important life processes.

Box 1 Life Processes.

Feeding	plants can make their own food, but animals eat plants and/or other animals.
Getting energy	living cells break down food to get energy.
Excretion	waste substances can't be used by the body, so have to be got rid of.
Reproduction	producing a new generation means life will go on in the future.
Growth	as living things grow they increase in size and their bodies develop.
Movement	living things move parts of their bodies, some can move from place to place too.
Being sensitive	detecting changes in the surroundings.

Picture 2 How humans get energy.

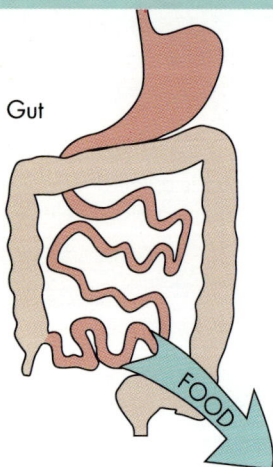

The **gut** is really a food processor that breaks down food. The food particles pass into the bloodstream and to all cells of the body. Our **lungs** are organs that help to get air into the body. Oxygen from the air is carried by **blood** to all the cells. **Respiration** happens in the cells. It is the release of energy from food.

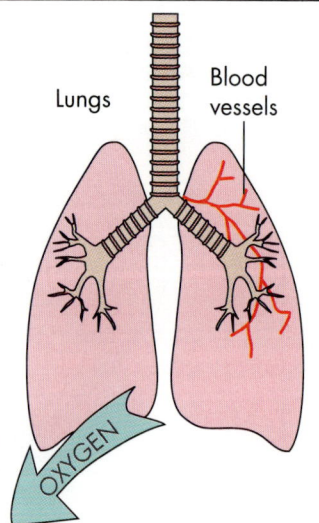

Gut

Lungs

Blood vessels

FOOD

OXYGEN

Food + Oxygen → ENERGY + carbon dioxide + water

Getting energy

To get energy you need a **food supply** and **oxygen**. When the oxygen combines with food, energy is released. This process is called **respiration**. Plants carry out respiration too.

Reproduction

At the start of the 1990's the human population was around 5200 million, but by 2000 it's expected to be 6000 million. Reproduction is responsible for this huge increase. All living things reproduce – otherwise they would die out.

Growth

You probably are getting taller and heavier as you read this. Like most animals you'll stop growing when you're adult.

Plants go on growing all their lives – think of a tree, for example.

Other changes happen as young animals become adults. You can read more about the changes that happen to humans in topic 2.11.

Picture 3 This is an adult Herdwick sheep. You can tell its age by the length of its horns.

Movement

Parts of your body are moving all the time – when you breathe and your heart beats. **Muscles** make animals move. Plants can't move from place to place, but they can move bits of themselves.

Being sensitive

How living things behave depends on them being **sensitive to** changes which happen around them. **Sense organs** like eyes and ears help living things to survive. Plants are sensitive too. For example, they grow towards sources of water and light.

Picture 4 Keeping an eye on things.

QUESTIONS

1 Thomas has a toy monkey. How can you tell it's not alive?

Picture 5

2 (a) Copy this flowchart into your book. Fill in the spaces using words from the list below.

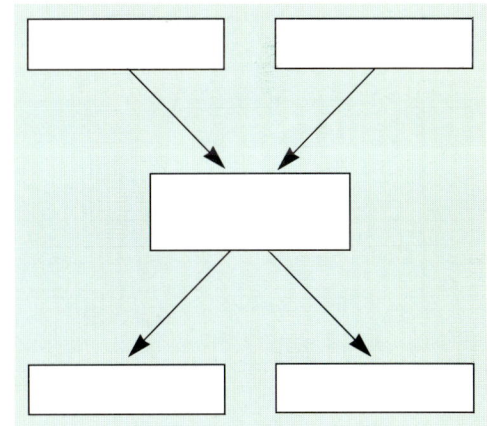

energy, food, waste, oxygen, food and oxygen combine
(b) What is the name for this process?

3 (a) What are your main senses?
(b) For each of the senses named in (a), say how you think it is important for your survival.

39

2.11 All change

Our bodies undergo constant change from the moment we're born to the moment we die. At times like puberty, some of the changes are quite dramatic. They change how we feel as well as how we look.

At **puberty** the body begins the change from child into young adult. These body changes mean that young adults can become parents.

What's the difference?

Picture 1 Body changes.

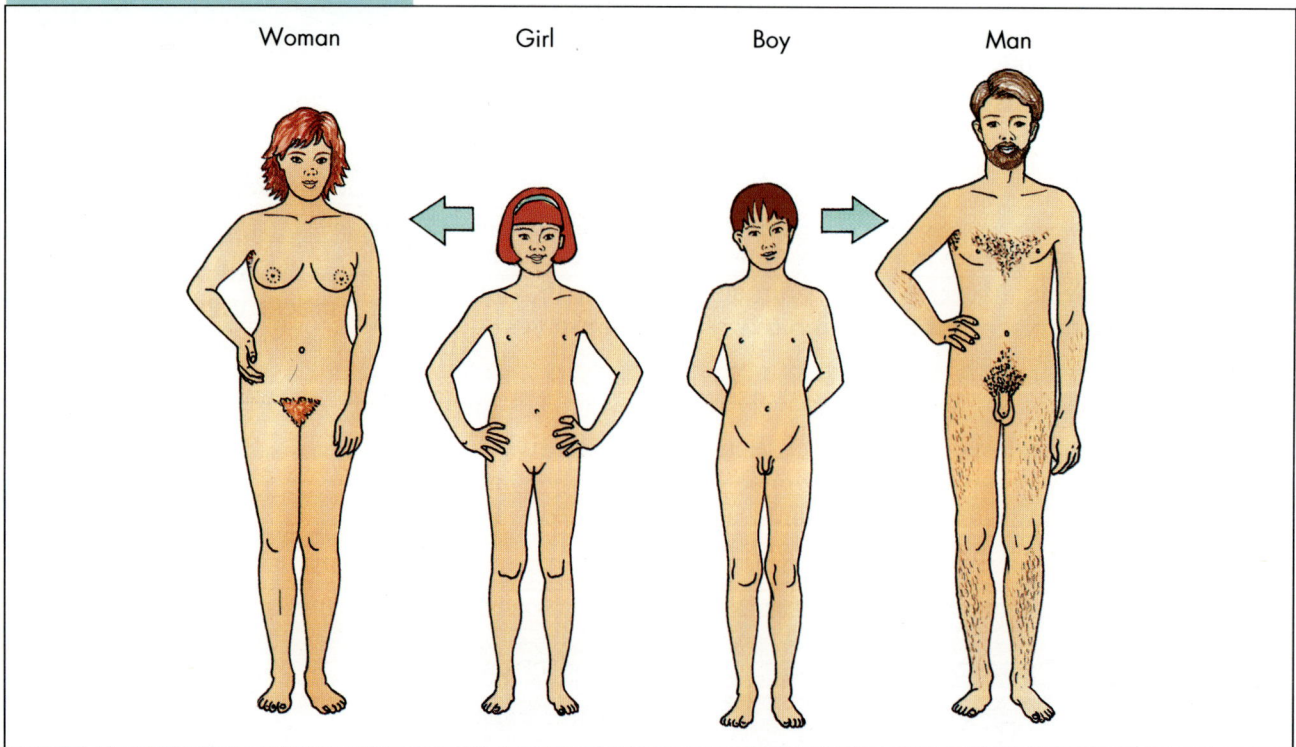

Woman Girl Boy Man

Changes happen *inside* the body too. The ovaries inside a girl start to produce **eggs** and her **periods** start. A boy's **testes** (sometimes called 'balls') start to make **sperms**.

Everyone's different

People reach puberty at different ages. Girls usually reach puberty when they're between 10 and 14 years old, while boys mature at 12 to 16 years old. Puberty happens when the body starts making chemicals called **hormones**. Hormones can affect our moods. Young people sometimes feel unsure of themselves and often get called 'moody'.

The sex organs

Pictures 2a and 2b shows the adult sex organs.

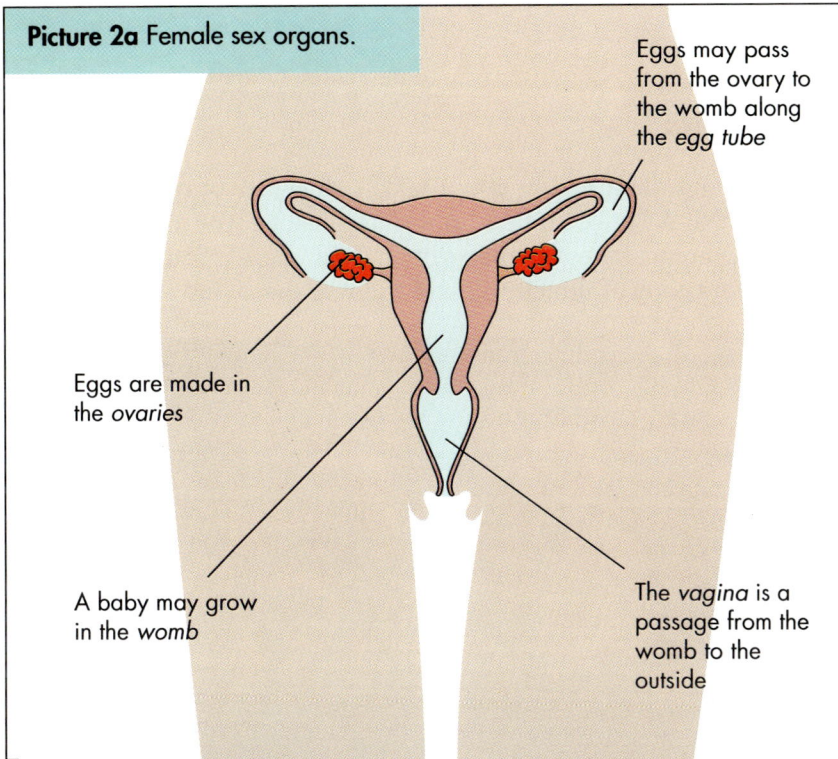

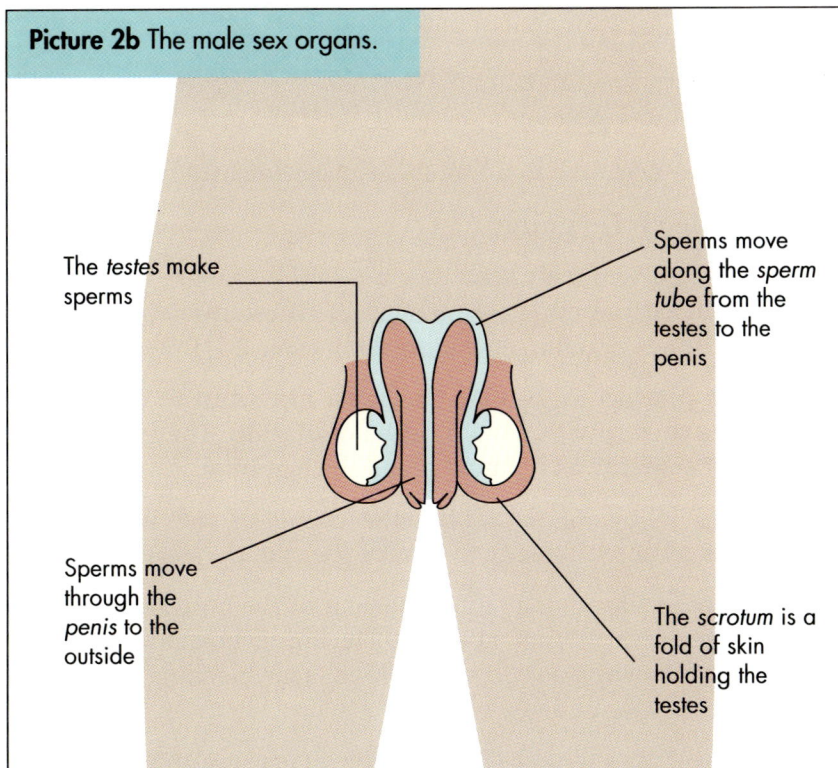

Picture 2a Female sex organs.

Eggs may pass from the ovary to the womb along the *egg tube*

Eggs are made in the *ovaries*

A baby may grow in the *womb*

The *vagina* is a passage from the womb to the outside

Picture 2b The male sex organs.

The *testes* make sperms

Sperms move along the *sperm tube* from the testes to the penis

Sperms move through the *penis* to the outside

The *scrotum* is a fold of skin holding the testes

1 What is the time of life called when the body begins changing from childhood to adulthood?

2 What changes happen during puberty to
(a) a girl's ovaries?
(b) a boy's testes?

3 Draw up a table of all the differences that happen to boys and girls during puberty. Use these headings:

Changes that happen to boys	Changes that happen to girls and boys	Changes that happen to girls

4 What chemicals in the body bring about the body changes described in question 3?

2.12 The human life cycle

Stages in life

Every minute of each day about 6000 babies are born somewhere in the World. At the other end of human life people are dying too. These are both stages in the human **life cycle**. Picture 1 shows three generations of the family and their stages of life.

Picture 1 The Jones family.

Keeping life cycles going

After puberty, a woman's body has a monthly pattern of changes called the **menstrual cycle** (see picture 2). These monthly changes happen in the sex organs (see picture 2a in topic 2.11).

The ovaries produce eggs. One egg is set free from an ovary into the egg tube each month. This is called **ovulation**. The egg may be fertilised by a sperm, as it passes along the egg tube.

In the days following ovulation, the lining of the womb gets thicker. This means it is ready to receive the egg, if it gets fertilised.

But if it's not fertilised, the egg passes out of the body. The thicker lining of the womb is not needed. The lining breaks down and passes out of the vagina with some blood. This bleeding is called a **period**. It lasts several days.

Topic 2.13 describes what happens when an egg is fertilised.

Picture 2 A monthly cycle.

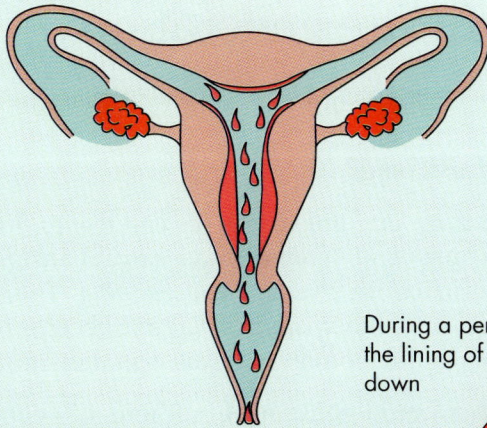

During a period blood is lost as the lining of the womb breaks down

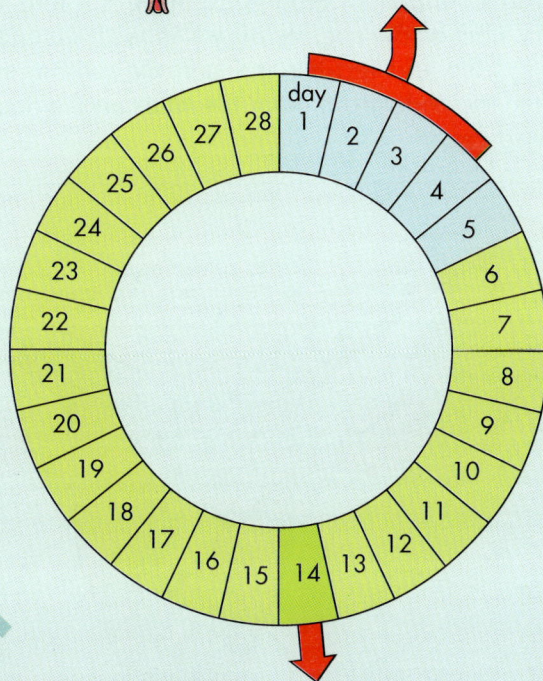

The lining of the womb gets thicker, ready to receive an egg if it gets fertilised

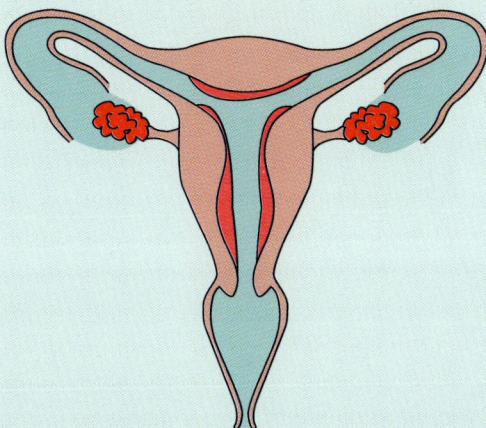

day 1 2 3 4 5 6 7 8 9 10 11 12 13 14 15 16 17 18 19 20 21 22 23 24 25 26 27 28

During ovulation an egg is set free from one ovary

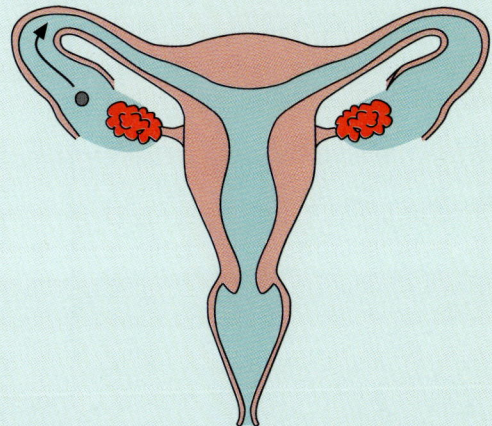

QUESTIONS

1 Think about your own family or a friend's family.
Write a list of
(a) relatives in your generation.
(b) relatives in your parents' generation.
(c) relatives in your grandparents' generation.

How is life different at each of these stages in life?

2 Shu-Li's last period started on 23rd February. It lasted 4 days. Use a calendar to help you work out the most likely date when
(a) she will ovulate next.
(b) her next period will start.

3 (a) What changes happen to the womb in the last half of the menstrual cycle?
(b) Why do a woman's periods stop when she is pregnant?

43

2.13 The future generation

How is an egg fertilised?

'*Having sex*' or '*making love*' are words we can use to describe what happens when a man and woman have **sexual intercourse**. The feelings they experience are pleasant and exciting. The man's penis gets stiff and erect and the woman's vagina becomes moist. The man puts his penis in the woman's vagina and they move together.

The penis squirts a liquid containing millions of sperms into the vagina. One of the sperms may join with an egg as it passes along the egg tube and fertilise it. Then the woman becomes **pregnant**. The genetic code from both the man and woman combine in the fertilised egg.

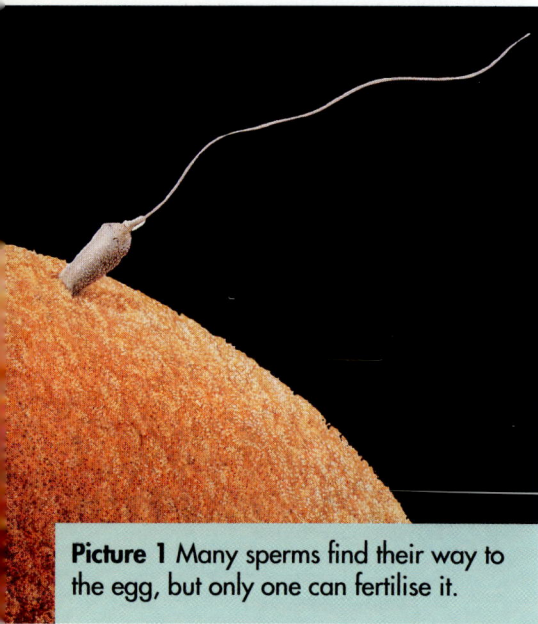

Picture 1 Many sperms find their way to the egg, but only one can fertilise it.

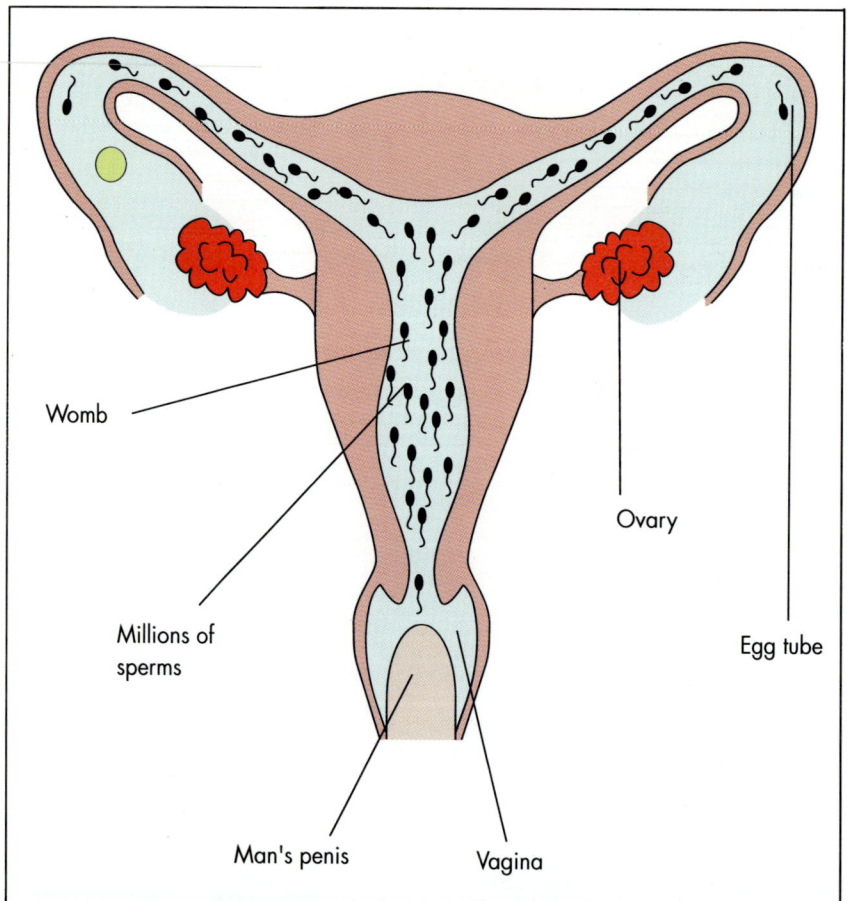

Picture 2 Sperms are squirted into the vagina and swim through the womb to the egg tubes.

What happens to a fertilised egg?

As the fertilised egg continues its journey along the egg tube, it divides into a small ball of cells. This lodges in the lining of the womb, and is called an **embryo** or developing baby. It grows inside a bag of watery liquid that fills the womb. The bag acts as a cushion to protect the embryo from damage.

Picture 3 This is a photograph of a 12-week embryo. All the organs have formed and the baby's heart has already started to beat. It has a mass of about 28 g.

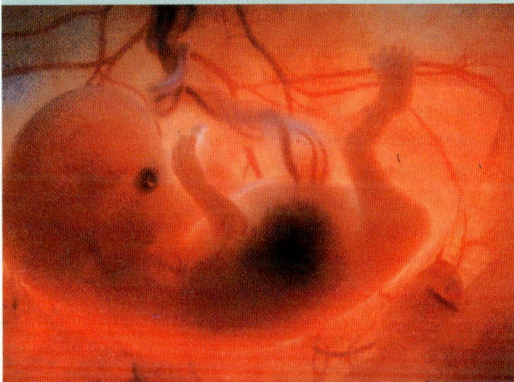

The developing embryo gets a supply of food and oxygen through a special organ called the **placenta**. The placenta develops from the lining of the womb. A cord called the **umbilical cord** joins the baby to the placenta. As the baby's blood moves through the placenta, all the substances it needs pass in from the mother's blood.

Picture 3–5 show some stages of the baby's development. After 40 weeks the baby is born.

QUESTIONS

1 Why do you think that sexual intercourse is also called '*making love*'?

2 Where is an egg fertilised?

3 What happens to a fertilised egg
(a) before it reaches the womb?
(b) when it first reaches the womb?

4 Nicotine (from tobacco) and alcohol can pass from the mother's blood to the baby, through the placenta.
(a) How might these substances affect the baby?
(b) A pregnant woman should not take any medicines without asking her doctor first. Suggest a reason why not.

Picture 4 At 24 weeks the baby's body is just fully formed. It weighs about 500 g.

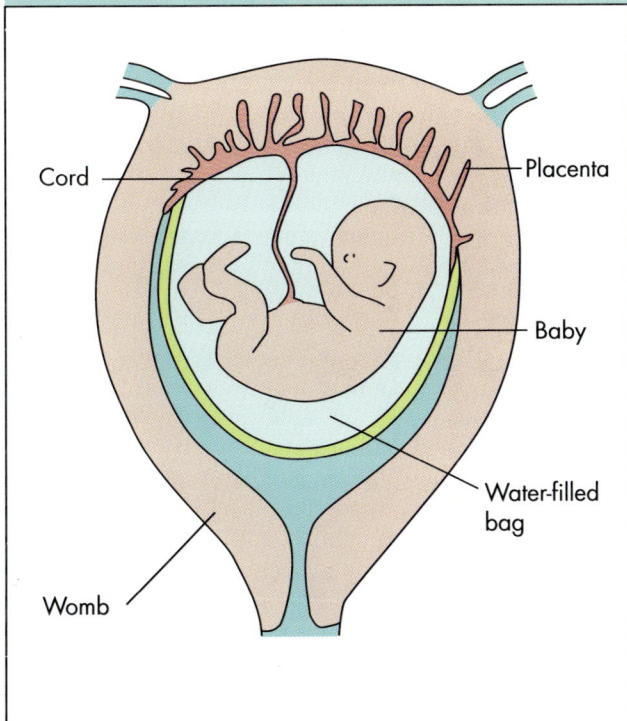

Cord — Placenta — Baby — Water-filled bag — Womb

Picture 5 At 40 weeks the baby fills the womb. It weighs around 3.4 kg and is ready to be born.

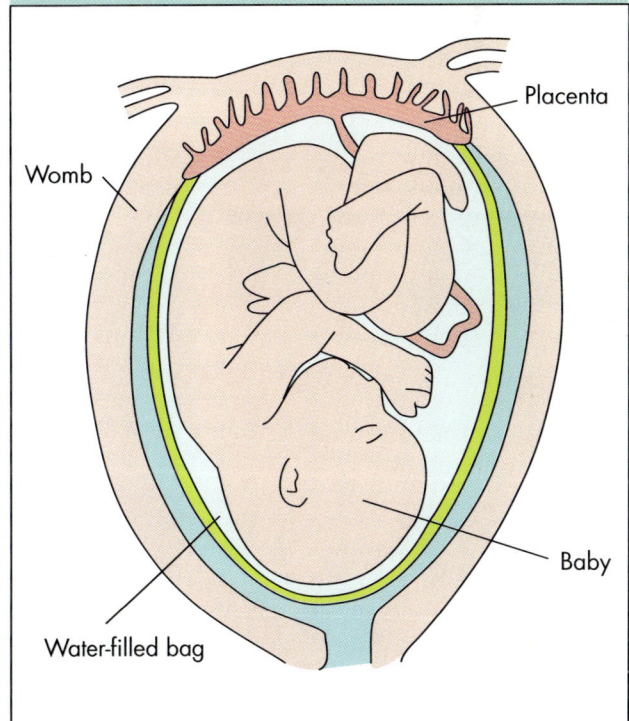

Womb — Placenta — Baby — Water-filled bag

Picture 1 Keeping healthy is important for pregnant women.

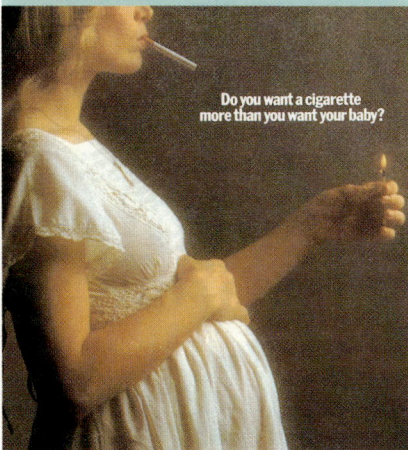

Do you want a cigarette more than you want your baby?

Picture 2 Close encounters.

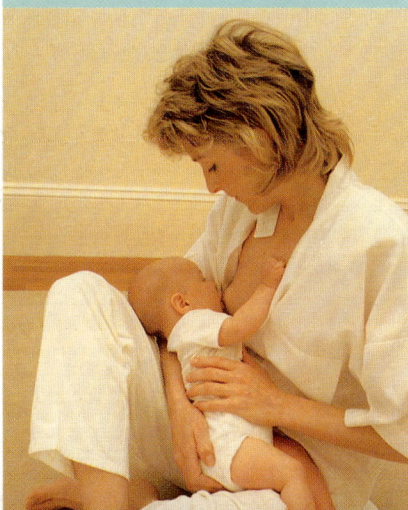

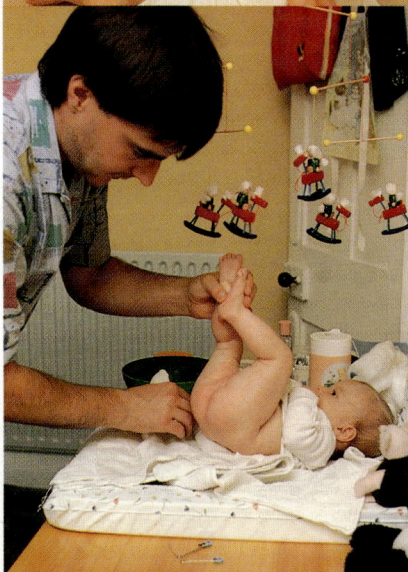

2.14 Caring

When does it all start?

Having a baby is a big responsibility. There will be many changes in **life style** for the parents, especially if it's their first baby.

One important decision that parents may have to make early on, is whether they will both go out to work after the baby is born.

The new baby

A **newborn baby** is helpless and needs constant care. At first a baby needs to be fed about every three hours. Parents spend a lot of time changing nappies, bathing the baby and cuddling it. In fact, humans spend more time caring for their young than any other animal.

After the birth, a mother's breasts begin to produce milk. Milk is the only food the baby has for the first few months of its life. Babies can be fed on cow's milk from a bottle but there's a lot to be said for breast-feeding. Breast milk is a perfect food ready at all hours and contains things that help protect the body against disease.

Growing and learning

Mathew in picture 3 is special. He is a Down's Syndrome child and will need much care and help from his parents and society. He may never learn to do all the things that other children can. Most childhood learning is done by **copying** other people. Parents are very important in this process.

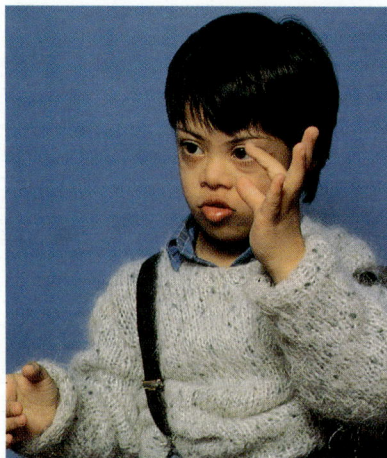

Picture 3 Mathew needs extra special care.

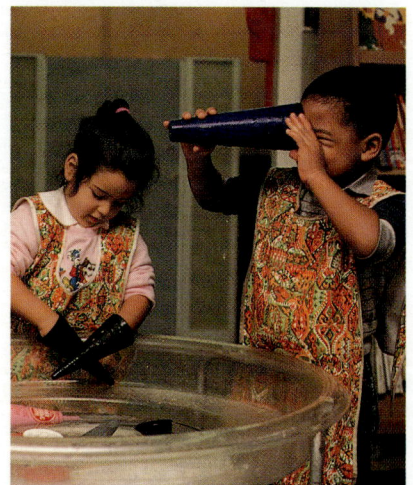

Picture 4 Learning through play.

Do you remember when? ...

Developing full adult skills takes about a quarter of our lives. Although we often remember the first time a child shows a new skill, development is actually a continuous process. Picture 5 shows the pattern of development for an average child.

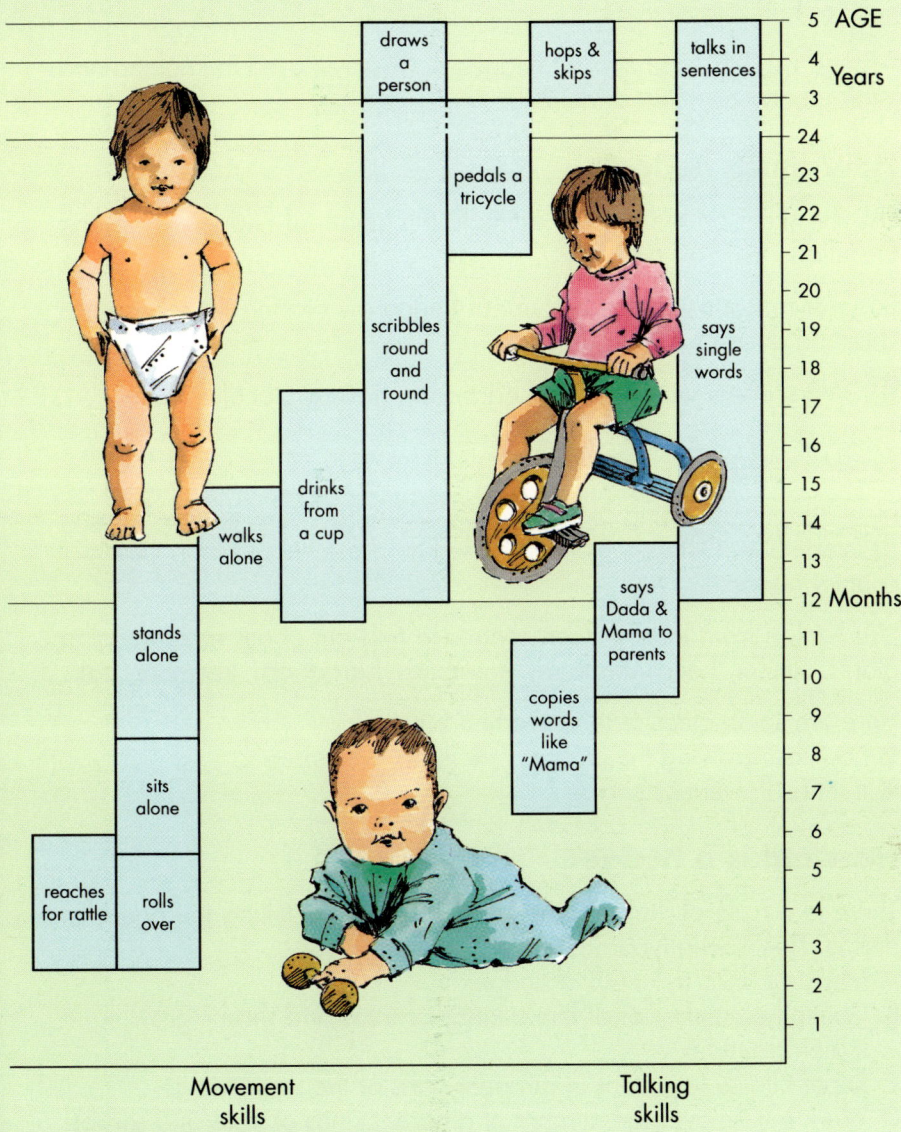

Picture 5 Some moments to remember.

Keeping in touch

It's important that youngsters get some freedom and learn to be **independent** before they leave home. But it can be a stormy time if teenagers want more freedom than their parents think they should have. Talking problems over helps people to understand each others' point of view.

1 Suggest ways in which a couple's life style might change after they have a baby.

2 Why do some parents prefer (a) breast feeding a baby? (b) bottle feeding a baby?

3 Why is it important for parents to cuddle a baby?

4 Are you still learning skills by copying others?

5 When does most development happen for (a) movement skills? (b) language skills?

6 Write a short story involving a conversation between teenager and a parent. Use this sentence as a starting point —

'You won't let me grow up – I'm not a child any more!'

A homely hedge

A hedge is home for many different plants and animals. It can offer shelter from the weather and enemies. It's a place to build a web or a nest, or find a tasty meal.

Around 82,277 kilometres of hedgerow were removed in England and Wales, between 1984 and 1990.

How much hedge?

Use the scale on the map to estimate the length of hedgerow around the village in 1960 and 1990.

Suggest reasons why the amount of hedgerow around the village has changed over the time.

1 What effect would losing hedgerows have on local wildlife?

New hedges

New hedges are being planted, often around gardens in new housing developments. Different plants are used for these hedges than the older country hedges.

Use leaflets from local garden centres to find out about some hedging plants: **conifer, beech, firethorn, hawthorn, blackthorn, lavender, box.**

Here are some ideas of things to find out:
● how fast growing the plant is   ● if it is evergreen
● if it has flowers or berries.

How old is a hedge?

There is a 'rule of thumb' that seems to work for telling the age of a hedge. This is what you do:
A Measure a 27 m length of hedge.
B Count the number of different kinds of trees and shrubs growing in it (not bramble).
C Repeat this a few times in different parts of the same hedge.
D Work out an average number of different kinds of trees and shrubs.
E Now multiply this number by 100 to tell you how old the hedge is.

2 Why do you think that older hedges have a greater variety of trees and shrubs growing in them?

3 Do you think there is a difference between the variety of animals living in an older hedge and in a newly planted conifer hedge? How would you find out?

Picture 1 A small section of a village map, showing hedges, 1960.

Scale (m)
0 10 20

Picture 2 The same village, 1990.

Scale (m)
0 10 20

Key
house   road
fields   hedges

48

Beetles and hedges

Picture 3 shows the number of ground beetles found, by setting pitfall traps overnight 1 metre apart along a transect through a hedge.

4 Where are most ground beetles found along this transect?

Suggest reasons why different numbers of ground beetles were found in each pitfall trap.

Picture 3 Where are the ground beetles?

8   3   1   6   0

Eek! It's a mouse, or is it?

Picture 4 Small mammals – similar but not the same.

A Use the key below to name **a**, **b** and **c**.

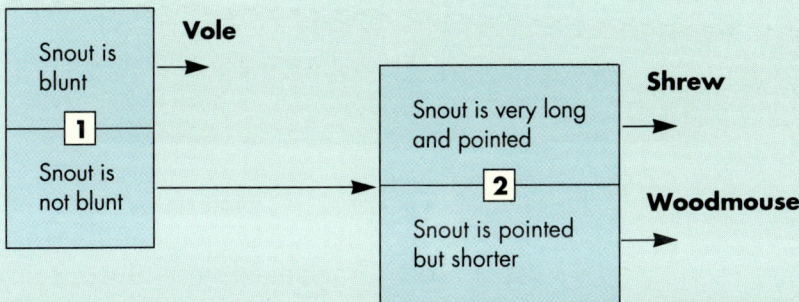

B Fill in table 1. The key above and picture 4 will help you.

Animal	Ears	Snouts	Tails	Food
Shrew				Carnivorous (meaty things)
Woodmouse				Nuts, seeds, roots
Vole				Nuts, seeds, roots

Table 1

C Try writing a key like the one in part A (above), using two other features, for example: tail length, ear shape or food.

D Do you know what small mammals live near you? Talk about this with a partner. Plan how you would find out.

⚠ (**Don't** do an investigation without asking your teacher first.)

49

Topic 3 ■ MATERIALS AND MIXTURES

3.1 Materials around us

Look at picture 1 of a science class at work in a laboratory.

Picture 1 A science class at work.

You can see a variety of **materials**. Some of them are **natural**, like *wood*, *wool* and *rubber*. They have not been changed very much from the natural state in which they were found. We use these materials almost as we find them. Can you spot any more materials like this?

Other materials are manufactured or **man-made** like *plastics*, *metals* and *glass*. But you may not have realised that the clothing worn by the students is likely to contain man-made *fibres*. These fibres are often coloured by man-made *dyes*. You should be able to find more examples of manufactured materials in picture 1.

We can sort most of the materials in picture 1 into one of the five important groups, **glass**, **fibres**, **ceramics**, **metals** and **plastics**, shown in table 1.

You can learn more about these materials in the rest of this topic.

Table 1 The five groups of materials.

Type of materials	Example
Glass	Spectacle lenses
Fibres	Wool
Ceramics	Crockery
Metals	Cutlery
Plastics	

Raw materials

Some natural materials are of little use to us in themselves. But they may be very important as **raw materials**. We can use them to make other materials. *Crude oil* is a very important raw material, which you can read more about in topic 3.8. We make from it many of the materials which we use in our everyday lives.

Try to identify the valuable raw materials which are being produced in pictures 2 and 3. What are they used for?

Picture 2

Picture 3

We shall have a lot more to say about raw materials and their uses in other parts of this book.

Materials and the way we live

Modern societies like ours are very dependent on manufactured materials. We take them for granted in our everyday lives. Imagine what life would be like without them!

Suppose we carried out a survey of materials in a society very different from our own. What would we find? Look at pictures 4 and 5.

Picture 4 Eskimos.

Picture 5 Wandering herdsmen in Africa.

These people are much less dependent on manufactured materials. They make far greater use of natural materials than people in Britain. Their style of life is very different from ours!

QUESTIONS

1 Find as many examples as you can of natural and man-made materials in your school laboratory. Write down their names in a table like this:

Natural materials	Man-made material
Wood	Glass

2 Some laboratory floors have a vinyl (plastic) covering, while others are made from wood blocks.
Describe some of the advantages and disadvantages of using each of these materials to cover a laboratory floor.

3 What are the names of the raw materials being produced in pictures 2 and 3? Describe as many uses as you can for each raw material.

4 Find out how we make
(a) glass.
(b) a ceramic material like pottery.

5 Write down some of the benefits and problems of living in a society where man-made materials are used a lot.

51

Picture 1 Flint tools from the Stone age.

Picture 2 A weapon from the bronze age.

Picture 3 An Iron Age hill fortress, in Dorset.

3.2 Putting materials to work

Ancient materials

People have been using materials obtained from the earth throughout history. In the Stone Age, they discovered flint, a hard rock that breaks to form sharp edges. From this, they made tools and weapons.

Archaeologists have dug up remains which show that early people made pottery by baking clay. They used bone to make needles. Cave paintings show that their tools were also made from wood, but there is little archaeological record of this.

About 7000 years ago, man discovered **metals**. This was a great step forward for civilisation because metals were more useful than anything known before. They were hard like stone but were also flexible and strong. They could be hammered into a great variety of shapes without breaking. It was not long before man learned how to melt metals and cast them into moulds.

By the end of the Bronze Age, 3500 years ago, people could use metals like gold, silver, copper and tin. But these metals were not hard or strong enough for many practical uses. Iron was much more useful for making tools and weapons because of its greater strength and hardness.

We often speak in science about the *property* of a material. By this, we mean the way the material behaves. **Strength**, **hardness** and **flexibility** are all important and useful properties of iron.

During the Iron Age, people discovered many new ways of using these properties to make better tools and weapons.

Alloys and modern materials

In the Bronze Age, people found that pure copper could not be used to make weapons with sharp edges because it was too soft. They solved this problem by mixing copper with small amounts of another metal, tin. This produced bronze, an **alloy** of copper and tin. It is harder than either copper or tin and can be sharpened.

Picture 4 Alloys used in a motor car.

Key:
1 Spark plug: barium alloy
2 Carburettor: aluminium alloy
3 Battery: lead/antimony
4 Bodywork: mild steel
5 Door handle: zinc alloy
6 Exhaust: iron/aluminium alloy
7 Wheel: magnesium alloy
8 Engine block: cast iron
9 Bearings: lead/tin

QUESTIONS

1 Why did Stone Age people find flint so useful?

2 Archaeologists have found a lot of evidence that ancient people made tools from the bones of animals. They probably used wood as well but archaeologists have found little evidence of this. How do you explain this?

3 Why are so many different alloys used in a motor car?

4 Choose two of the substances in the list taken from the *Guinness Book of Records*.
(a) Suggest a use for each of the substances.
(b) Explain the link between the use of each substance and its special property.

Bronze was probably the first alloy to be made. Today there are thousands! You can find quite a lot in picture 4.

Why are there so many different alloys?

Elsewhere in this book, you can read how man has learned to adapt and transform many other materials for a variety of uses. Table 1 shows some entries from the *1991 Guinness Book of Records*. It shows materials obtained by scientists and technologists with record-breaking properties!

Table 1

Property	Name of substance
Highest melting point	Tantalum carbide (3990°C)
Hardest	Diamond
Lightest solid	Silica aerogel (1 cm³ weighs 0.005 g)
Lightest gas	Hydrogen (1 cm³ weighs 0.00009 g)
Finest powder	Solid helium
Smelliest	Probably ethyl mercaptan (smells something like rotting cabbage)
Most absorbent	H-span or Super Slurper (holds 1300 times its own mass of water)

3.3 Materials from the earth

Today, we can get many different raw materials from the earth for building and manufacturing. Many **rocks** and **minerals** found in the UK are used as raw materials. Look at the graph in picture 1.

Picture 1 This bar chart shows the masses of different minerals produced in the UK in 1989.

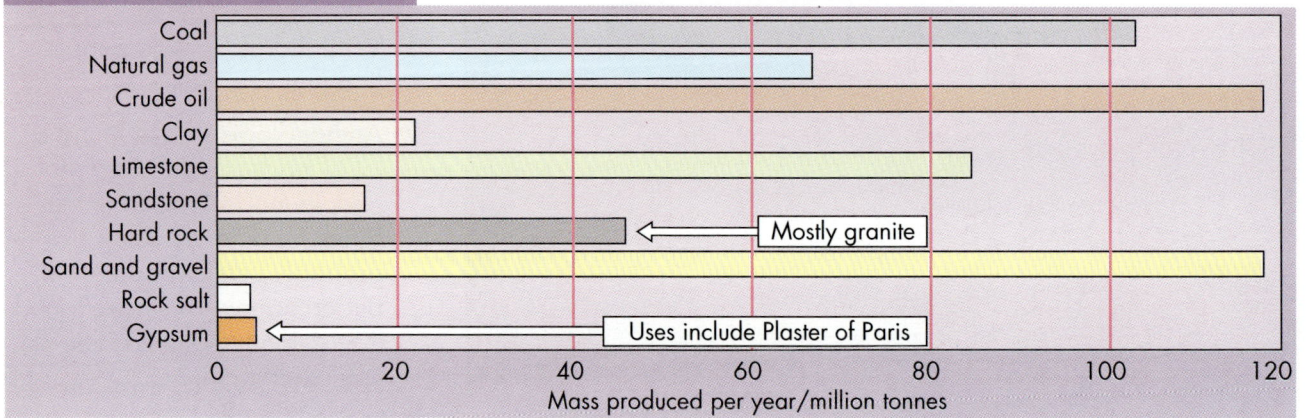

Mass produced per year/million tonnes

Let us see how some of these raw materials are used.

Coal

Coal is used to produce energy. In the late 1980s, it provided about a third of the energy which is needed in the UK. It is also used to make **coke**, a smokeless fuel.

Picture 2 Three ways of mining coal.

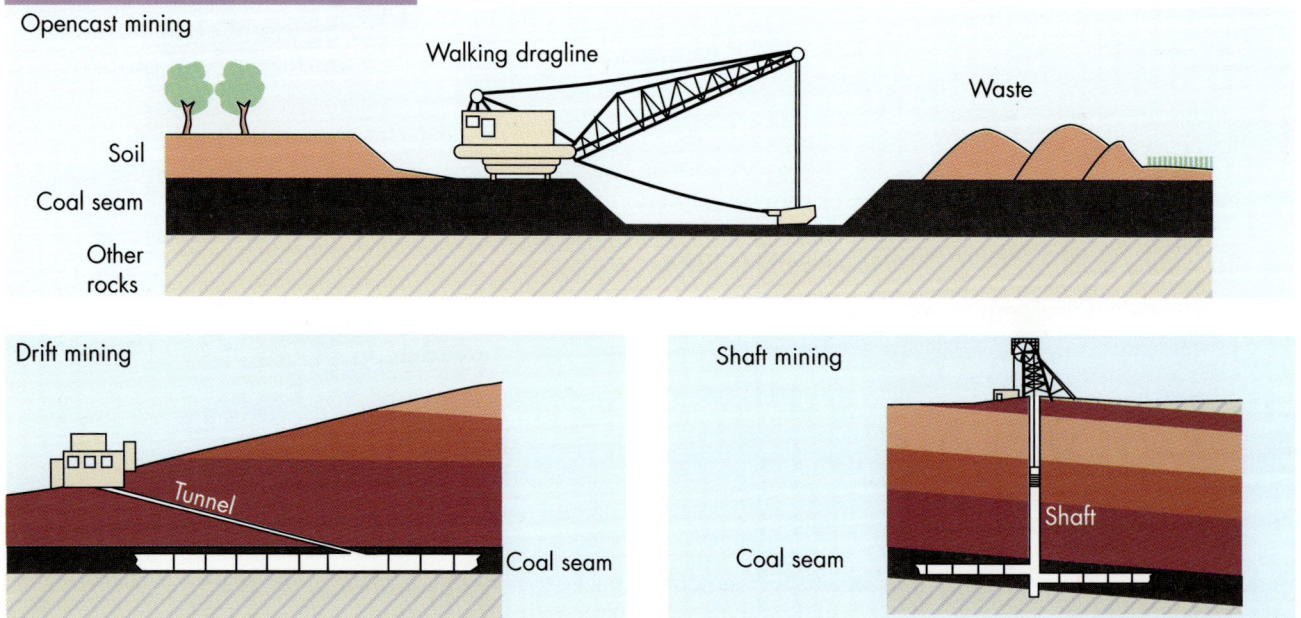

Opencast mining

Walking dragline

Waste

Soil

Coal seam

Other rocks

Drift mining

Tunnel

Coal seam

Shaft mining

Shaft

Coal seam

There are now far fewer coal mines in Britain than there used to be. Getting coal from deep mines can be costly. Can you suggest cheaper ways of obtaining coal? Picture 2 may help.

It is important to remember what impact mining activities will have on the *environment*. You can learn more about this in topic 3.5.

Picture 3 Limestone outcrops in the UK.

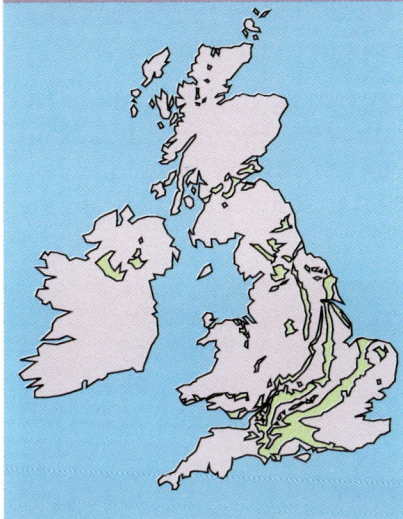

Picture 4 The uses of limestone in 1987.

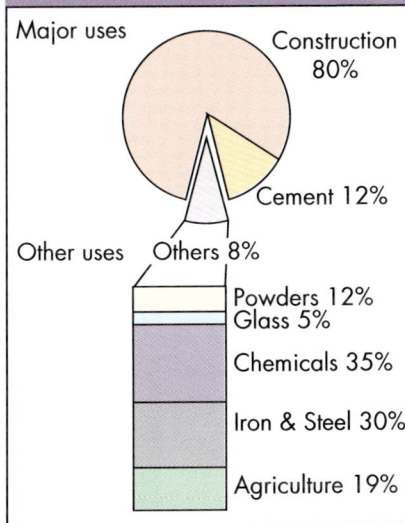

Major uses
Construction 80%
Cement 12%
Other uses   Others 8%
Powders 12%
Glass 5%
Chemicals 35%
Iron & Steel 30%
Agriculture 19%

Limestone

Limestone is one of the most common rocks in Britain as picture 3 shows. You can see from the barchart in picture 1 that it is very widely used as a raw material. Some of its varied uses are shown in the pie chart (picture 4).

The demand for limestone for road-making and building has been rapidly increasing during this century. To meet this demand, more quarries have had to be opened. This again leads to environmental problems. What are these problems?

Iron Ore

Iron ore is one of the raw materials we need to make steel. The first step in steel-making is to get iron from its ore. We do this by heating a mixture of iron ore, coke and limestone in a furnace. Hot air is blasted through the furnace and the mixture produces a different substance, iron. One substance changes into another one. This is an example of a **chemical change**.

The iron from the blast furnace goes to a steel-making furnace. Here more chemical changes turn iron into steel.

Picture 5 shows a summary of the changes which take place when iron ore changes into steel.

Picture 5 Steel-making.

1 Coal is only one of the minerals which is used in this country to produce energy. Name two others.

2 Gypsum is one of the minerals shown in the bar graph in picture 1. From gypsum, we can make Plaster of Paris. What is this used for?

3 Which do you think is the cheapest method of mining coal? Explain why you think this is the cheapest. Describe any disadvantages of this method of getting coal.

4 Why do you think the demand for limestone has been rapidly increasing during the present century?

5 What are the environmental problems which limestone quarrying brings? How can these problems be reduced?

6 Look again at the steps involved in the conversion of iron ore into steel, shown in picture 5. Keeping in mind the raw materials needed for steel manufacture, where in the British Isles would you choose to build a steelworks? Explain your choice.

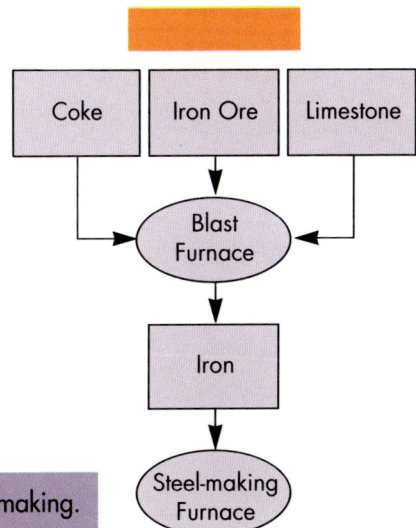

Coke | Iron Ore | Limestone
Blast Furnace
Iron
Steel-making Furnace

55

3.4 Building materials

Rocks and building stones

The map shows some of the many different types of rock you can find in the British Isles. What kind of rocks are there where you live?

Rocks are often used as **building stone**. In many parts of Britain, you find buildings made from stone which has been quarried locally. You can see some examples in the pictures 2a and 2b.

Picture 1 Geological map of British Isles.

Rock type

	Sands and clays
	Chalk
	Clays, sands, sandstone
	Limestone
	Coal measures
	Limestone, millstone grit
	Sandstone
	Shales and slates
	Gneiss, quartzite, schists
	Basalt and granite

Picture 2 Buildings made from local stone:
a Rhondda, Wales **b** Cotswolds, England.

Have you noticed any buildings made from local stone in your neighbourhood?

Brick

It is usually easier to find buildings made from **brick** than those made from local stone. Why is brick a more common building material than stone?

Bricks are cheap and come in handy shapes and sizes. They are made by heating clay to very high temperatures in a furnace. This is called *firing* the clay. You can see from the map that there are clays in many parts of Britain. Brickworks are mainly in areas where clay is most plentiful.

Look again at the map. Where would you be likely to find a brick-making industry?

Weathering

Look at the pictures 3a and 3b. Which of the building stones seems to have been changed more by the effects of weather?

Limestone gets worn away by the weather more than harder stone, like granite. This is called **weathering**. Rainwater is weakly acidic and slowly dissolves limestone. The limestone is changed into a different substance. When a substance changes into a different one, we call it a **chemical change**. So this is called **chemical weathering**.

Picture 3 a Granite houses in Cornwall. **b** A religious figure on Gloucester Cathedral.

This kind of weathering shapes the landscape in limestone areas. The results are often unusual, as you can see in picture 4.

Rocks are also weathered by wind, rain and changes of temperature. The rocks get broken into smaller bits, but its still the same substance. We call this **physical weathering**. Say some water soaks into a building stone. If the water freezes, it will expand and cause stresses and strains in the stone. Over a period of many years, the stone may break up.

This explains the condition of the stone wall shown in picture 5.

Picture 4 A limestone pavement.

Picture 5 Weathered stone wall.

QUESTIONS

1 Use the map in picture 1 to find the rock type(s) in the area where you live. Write down their name(s).

2 Again with the help of the map, find the areas in which you would be most likely to find brickworks. Write down the names of these areas and explain why you would expect to find brickmaking there.

3 Describe how the following features of the landscape might have been formed by weathering
(a) limestone pavements.
(b) scree slopes. (Slopes on mountain sides made of lots of loose pieces of rock).

4 Try to explain why brick is now a much more common building material than natural stones such as limestone and granite.

5 Weathering of limestone buildings is usually much worse in industrial areas than in the country. How do you explain this?

57

3.5 Opencast coalmining

Picture 1 Opencasting in progress.

Picture 2 Opencast site at East Merthyr.

Coal is often found in Britain in **seams** or layers which are quite close to the surface. Shallow coal can be worked cheaply by digging it out from the surface. This is called **opencast mining**. Why is it more expensive to get coal from deep mines? (Look back at topic 3.3 if you need help to answer this question.)

Although opencast coal is cheap to produce, the methods used to mine it may cause damage and disturbance in the local environment. Any plans to mine coal in this way need very careful thought. Work cannot begin until the local authority approves plans for the mine.

Here is an outline of plans for a large opencast coalmine in South Wales.

A The site

The area to be opencasted is on the eastern edge of Merthyr Tydfil. This is an industrial town of 60,000 people in South Wales. The site covers 315 hectares or 1.2 square miles. Part of this is moorland. The rest was once occupied by the Dowlais ironworks – the biggest in the World during the last century.

The site of the ironworks is now mostly derelict. It is covered in many places by slag from old iron and steel furnaces.

B Coal production

British Coal estimates that at least 7 million tonnes of coal will be taken from the site. The work of mining coal and of restoring the site will be spread over fifteen years.

C Transport

Picture 3 Heavy vehicle's wheels are washed before it leaves an opencast site.

There are no convenient rail links, so coal would have to be moved from the site by road.

D Land improvement

British Coal would restore the land. It would then be used for business and industrial development. Sports and leisure centres would be built for the local community.

Picture 4 Opencast site after restoration.

QUESTIONS

1 In what ways would the local people benefit from a scheme like this?

2 What problems would the local community face if the scheme went ahead?

3 Here is a list of groups of people with an interest in the scheme. Each one has strong views about it:

Friends of the Earth
Residents' Association
Town councillors
Local business people
Unemployed people in Merthyr
Road haulage companies
Local doctors
Hill farmers

Sort these groups into those for the scheme and those against it. Briefly explain why you think each group will be for or against the scheme.

4 The cost of restoring and developing the site after coalmining is finished will be enormous.

Where should the money come from? Who should pay?

59

Picture 1 Roman soldiers on the march. These soldiers received part of their pay as salt. This is the origin of the word, 'salary', which means 'salt money'.

Picture 2 Afloat in the Dead Sea.

Picture 3 An underground salt mine.

3.6 Salt

Salt is an important substance. It has been used since ancient times to preserve food. It is also an important part of our diet. In Britain, an adult needs to consume about 2 g of salt each day. More is needed in hot countries.

Where does salt come from?

A *Sea water* Sea water covers about 70% of the surface of our planet. The oceans contain a huge supply of salt. On average, about 35 g of salt is dissolved in every litre. In warmer parts of the World, the saltiness or **salinity** of sea water is often greater than this. In colder climates, the sea water will be less salty. Try to think why.

Some lakes are also salty or **saline**. One of the best known is the Dead 'Sea' in the Middle East desert. It contains about 250 g of salt dissolved in every litre. You don't have to be a great swimmer to stay afloat in a lake like this!

B *Ancient seas* Salt can also be obtained as **rock salt** from mines like the one shown in picture 3.

The salt in this mine was formed about 25 million years ago. Earlier, an ancient sea covered the area. The water in the sea gradually turned to vapour (evaporated). Salt was left behind.

Rock salt is mined about 150 metres below ground. As you can see from picture 4, this has been known to cause problems for the local residents!

Picture 4 Collapsed houses in Northwich.

How do we get pure salt?

A *From sea water* The salt in sea water is in **solution**. How would you get salt from the solution? In climates which are warmer than ours, sea water is pumped into large shallow lakes on the shore. Crystals of salt form as the water is evaporated by the Sun. Picture 5 shows the salt being 'harvested'.

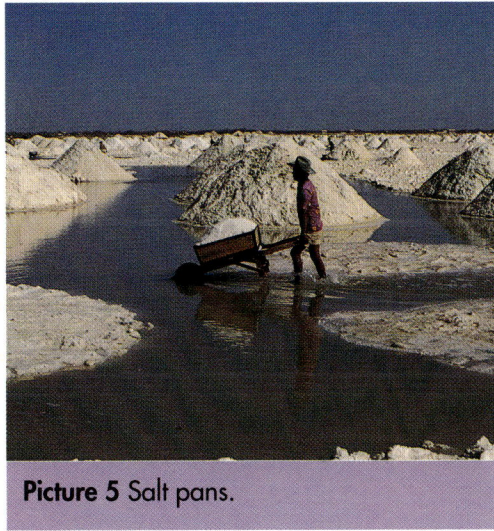

Picture 5 Salt pans.

B *From rock salt* Although rock salt is useful for clearing icy roads, it is too impure for most purposes. They get much purer salt by pumping water into boreholes drilled in the bed of rock salt. The salt dissolves and returns to the surface in a solution known as **brine** (picture 6).

You can get salt from the brine by evaporating the water. The salt is pure enough to be used in the food industry.

QUESTIONS

1 Why do you think Roman soldiers were paid 'salt-money'?

2 How much salt would you expect to get if you evaporated 10 litres of sea water?

3 Try to explain why the building in picture 4 has collapsed.

4 Why are the seas in the colder parts of the World less salty?

5 Why would you need to eat more salt if you lived in a very hot country?

6 Many countries in Africa have no coastline and no salt mines. Try to find out how the people of these countries make salt.

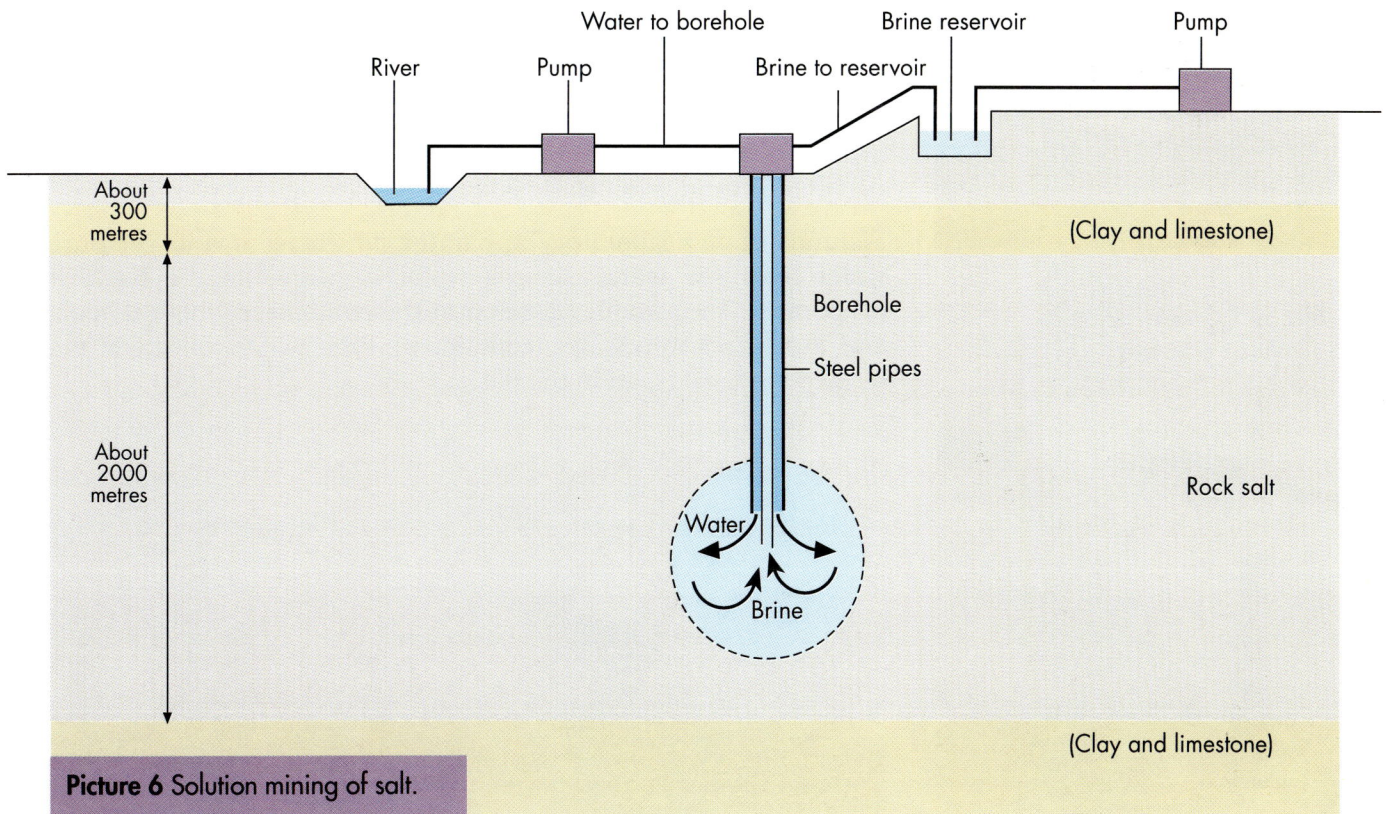

Picture 6 Solution mining of salt.

Picture 1 Vegetables being strained in a colander.

Picture 2 Air filter in a car engine.

Picture 3 Simple laboratory filtration apparatus.

Copper oxide

Copper sulphate solution

3.7 More ways to separate and purify things

Mixtures

A **mixture** contains substances which we can easily separate. Some familiar examples can be seen in the pictures 1 to 6. You are going to read about some of the methods we use to separate the substances in a mixture.

Filtering Pictures 1 to 3 show examples of filters. In each case, the filter separates one substance from another in a mixture. Picture 3 shows the apparatus we use in the laboratory for filtering.

For example, the colander separates the vegetables from the water in which they are cooked. Try to decide what the other filters do.

The substance which passes through the filter is called the **filtrate**. It is often a liquid but sometimes can be a gas (as in picture 2). The solid part of the mixture is left in the filter. It is called the **residue**.

Our water supply is filtered at the waterworks before it reaches our homes. Tapwater is the filtrate.

Distilling When you heat sea water, the water evaporates as vapour. If the vapour is cooled, it will **condense** to give pure water. This method of water purification is important in the Middle East. In that part of the World, fresh water is scarce but sea water is plentiful.

Picture 4 shows laboratory apparatus which we use to get pure water from sea water. As sea water is heated in the flask, it evaporates. The vapour passes into the **condenser** where it cools and turns back into water (condenses). Pure water collects in the receiver and salt is left in the flask.

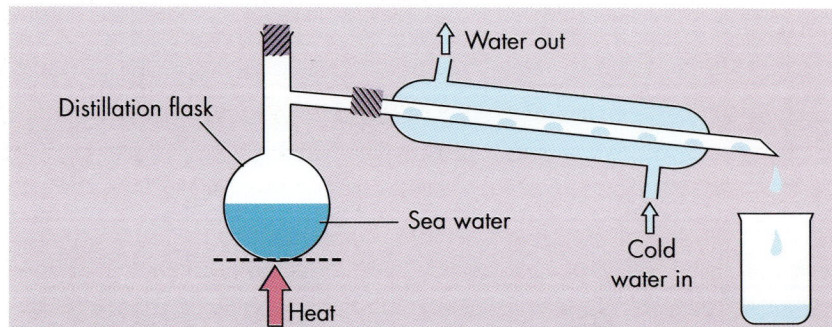

Picture 4 Distilling in the laboratory.

We call this process of evaporation followed by condensation, **distillation**.

Arabic Alchemy From about 600 AD, the country we now call Saudi Arabia was the centre of a very large, Islamic empire. The work of Arab scholars helped the early growth of science.

The Arabs believed that distilling materials from plants and animals would produce a substance called an **elixir**. They thought this would turn ordinary metals into gold. The search for an elixir was called **alchemy**. The Arab alchemists did not find an elixir, of course, but they did make many useful substances by distillation. Picture 5 shows the kind of apparatus they used.

Picture 5 Arab alchemists using distillation apparatus to produce an elixir.

The distillation products were used as medicines, perfumes and even food flavourings.

Chromatography The ink in your fountain pen or fibre tip often contains a mixture of coloured dyes. If you place a drop of black ink on something absorbent like filter paper, you can see these dyes begin to separate.

By adding a **solvent** like water to the paper, we get better separation of the dyes. Water dissolves some of the dyes and so some of the colours 'run'. These colours move with the water towards the edge of the paper, leaving others behind.

How many different dyes can you spot in the picture?

This method of separating is called **chromatography**.

QUESTIONS

1 Make a copy of the table below. The first row has been done for you. Complete the table by describing in the same way each of the filters shown in pictures 2 and 3.

Name of filter	Substances separated	
	Residue in filter	Filtrate
Colander	Vegetables	Water

2 (a) Purifying sea water by distillation needs a lot of energy.
  (b) The cost of purifying sea water in this way is not a problem in a Middle Eastern country like Saudi Arabia.

  Explain the statements in (a) and (b).

3 Compare pictures 4 and 5. The apparatus shown in each picture is used for distillation.

  Write down what you think happens in parts A, B and C of the apparatus shown in picture 5.

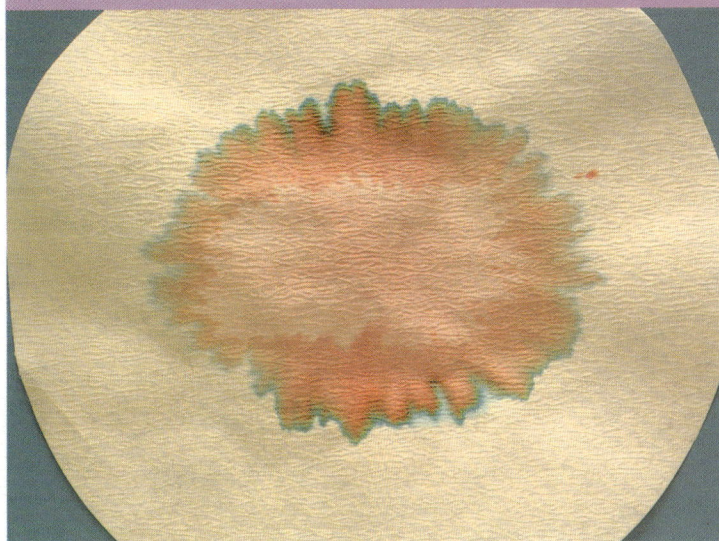

Picture 6 A simple example of paper chromatography.

63

3.8 Crude oil

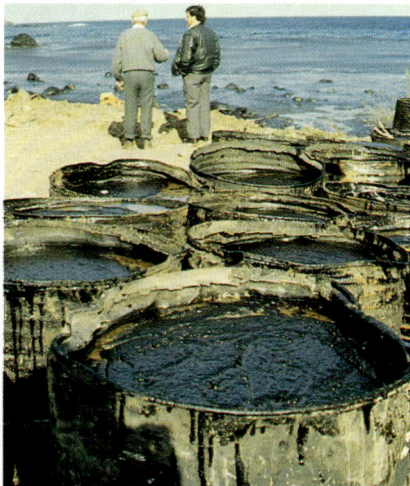

Picture 1 Crude oil.

What is crude oil?

Crude oil is a black smelly liquid. It is made from the remains of tiny plants and animals which settled on the sea floor. After being buried and squeezed by rocks for many millions of years, these remains were changed into crude oil. Because it was formed in this way, we call crude oil a **fossil fuel**.

Oil producers and users

Picture 2 shows which countries are the most important producers and users of oil. You can see that Britain is one of the smaller producers.

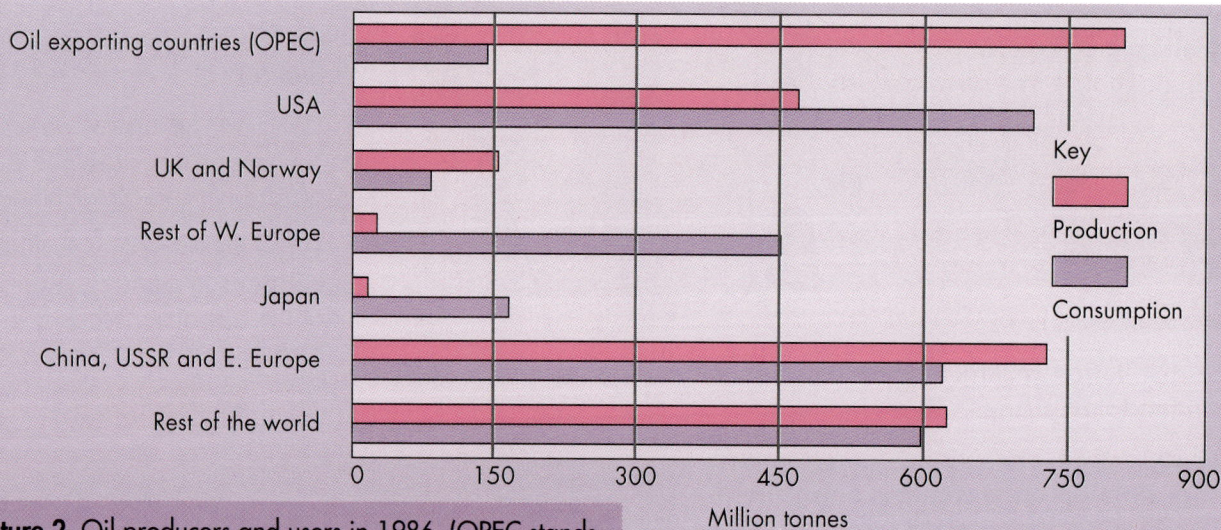

Key
Production
Consumption

Picture 2 Oil producers and users in 1986. (OPEC stands for Organisation of Petroleum Exporting Countries.)

Why is it so useful?

On its own, crude oil is useless. But we can make useful things *from* it. We get a variety of **fuels** from crude oil. Petrol, paraffin and diesel oil are the most common but there are many more. Fuels which come from crude oil are used for transport, for heating and in power stations.

In Britain about 90% of our crude oil is used for fuel. But we can also make useful *materials* from it. Substances called **petrochemicals** are made from crude oil. From these we can get plastics, paints, detergents and fibres.

Oil refining

Crude oil is a mixture of many different substances. We need to separate them to make the crude oil useful. They do this in an oil refinery by **fractional distillation**. They boil crude oil in a furnace. The vapours which come off go into a fractionating column like the one in picture 3.

As the vapours rise through the column, they cool. The column is hot at the bottom, cool at the top. Different vapours condense to liquids at different points in the column. Petrol condenses at a lower temperature than kerosene, for example. So, petrol collects further up the column than kerosene. Liquids of low *boiling point* condense near the top of the column. Near the bottom, liquids of much higher boiling point collect.

Many of the liquids (called **fractions**) which separate in this column are important as fuels.

One fraction you may not have heard of is **naphtha**. It is not used on its own, but we can use it to make useful gases like ethene. These gases can be changed into plastics like polythene. Ethene and other gases for making plastics are produced by **cracking** – heating naphtha in a furnace without air.

The gases we get from naphtha are used in the petrochemical industry to make plastics like the ones in picture 5.

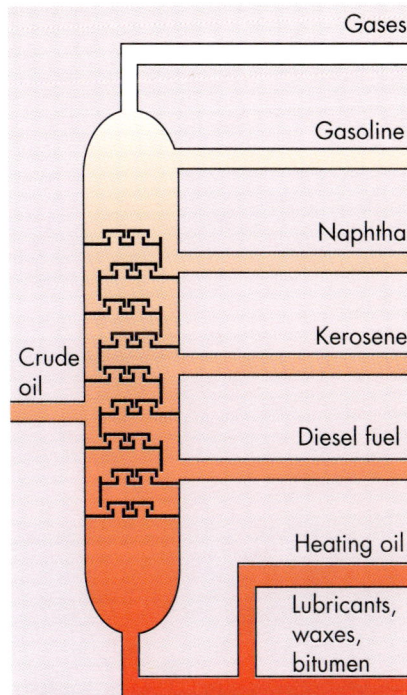

Picture 3 Fractional distillation of crude oil produces several useful products.

Picture 4 Aircraft being refuelled. Which crude oil fraction does it use?

Picture 5 Plastics used in packaging – made from crude oil.

QUESTIONS

1 Look at the barchart in picture 2. What is the largest oil producing area of the World?

2 Give an example of a country or part of the World which needs to import all or most of the oil it consumes.

3 Draw up a table to show one use for each of the crude oil fractions in picture 3. Some of these uses you will know already. You may need to do some research to find out about the others.

4 What happens to the vapours produced by boiling crude oil as they rise through a fractionating column?

5 Why does crude oil separate into fractions as vapour rises through the fractionating column?

Synthetic Materials

Many of the materials we use every day are man-made or **synthetic**. This is the story of the discovery of two important synthetic materials – **polythene** and **nylon**.

Polythene – the development of a modern plastic

Picture 1 Spitfires in action. Would they have succeeded without polythene?

Picture 2 Some everyday items made from polythene.

One of the most historic events in the development of synthetic materials took place in Britain just before World War 2. In 1933, Reginald Gibson and Eric Fawcett were working together at ICI. They were studying what happens to chemicals at high pressure.

By accident, they discovered that a white, waxy solid can be made from ethene gas when you heat it at very high pressure. The white solid was named polythene. It was light, flexible, tough and resistant to chemicals.

They investigated the electrical properties of polythene. At the same time *radar*, one of the most important scientific discoveries of World War 2, was being developed. Polythene proved to be an excellent insulator, ideal for coating radar cables. Without polythene, radar could not have been used in the defence of Britain until much later in the war.

Polythene is still used as a coating for wires and cables. Some of its many uses are shown in picture 2.

Nylon – the first synthetic fibre

Picture 3 shows the names some of the fibres used in our clothing. None of the fibres in the pictures are natural. They are all synthetic. Nylon was the first completely synthetic fibre.

Nylon was discovered in the USA in 1935 by Wallace Carothers. Unlike polythene, the nylon was *not* discovered by chance. It was the result of a careful research project to develop a fully synthetic fibre.

Until the 1930s, the only fibre for making ladies' stockings was silk. In 1939, thanks to Wallace Carothers' discovery, nylon stockings were marketed for the first time in the USA. They were much cheaper than silk stockings.

They say that four million pairs were sold in the first four days. Unfortunately, these stockings were soon in short supply. Most of the nylon made in the next six years was used to produce parachutes for the allied forces in World War 2.

Carothers was a brilliant chemist but often got very depressed. He never got over the death of his sister in 1936, and he committed suicide later in the same year. He did not live to see the birth of his own daughter or the enormous success of nylon products.

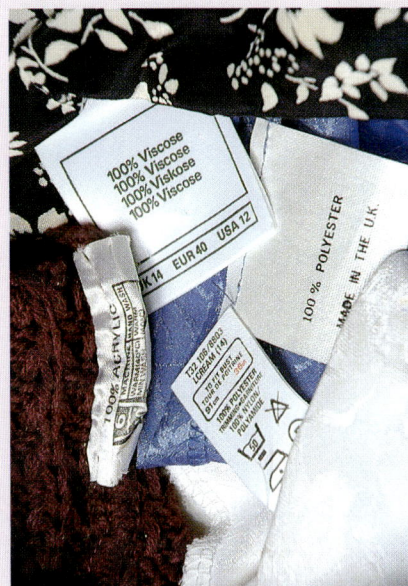

Picture 3 These labels show some of the fibres used to make clothes.

Picture 4 Wallace Carothers.

Either

Imagine you are a reporter working on an American newspaper in 1935. On 28 February, Wallace Carothers discovers nylon. Write a headline story for your newspaper about his achievement. Remember to describe to your readers the many ways in which you expect the new fibre to be used.

Try to produce your newspaper article on a word-processor or desktop publishing package if possible.

Or

Imagine you are one of the scientists at ICI who discovered polythene. Write a top-secret report of your discovery for the attention of the British Government of the 1930s. Describe as fully as you can

● the properties of polythene.
● some of its possible uses in wartime Britain.

Topic 4 ■ WATER AND THE WEATHER

4.1 Water fit to drink

Picture 1 Large pipes carry and empty pollutants into rivers.

Can you drink it?

Suppose you took a glass of water from a river. You probably wouldn't drink it because it would look dirty. You can see the dirt easily because it does not dissolve in the water.

What about seawater? It often *looks* clean. You still wouldn't drink it though, because it tastes salty. You can't see the salt because it dissolves in the water.

Picture 2 There is a lot of sea water available. Why don't we drink it?

Picture 3 Would you drink water from this lake?

Water in a lake also looks clean and it doesn't taste salty. It *might* be safe to drink, but it could still contain dissolved materials with no taste. **Bacteria** could also be present, which may be harmful.

Purifying water

The water that we use comes from rivers and reservoirs. Water authorities take this water and make it fit to drink. Picture 4 shows some of the stages at a Water Treatment Works.

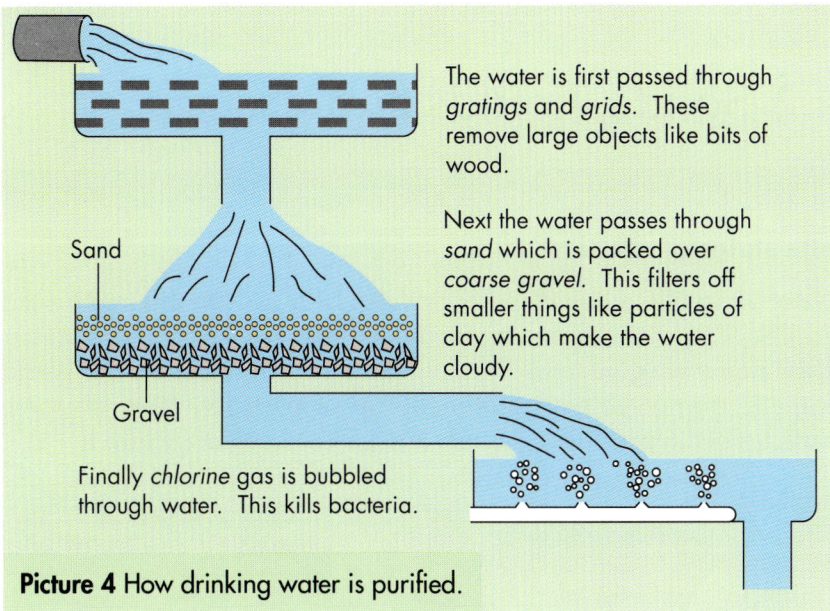

The water is first passed through *gratings* and *grids*. These remove large objects like bits of wood.

Next the water passes through *sand* which is packed over *coarse gravel*. This filters off smaller things like particles of clay which make the water cloudy.

Sand

Gravel

Finally *chlorine* gas is bubbled through water. This kills bacteria.

Picture 4 How drinking water is purified.

1 Colliford Lake was specially chosen to supply Cornwall with water. It was extended to make it bigger. Suggest why this particular lake might have been chosen.

2 What will be done to the water at Restormel Water Treatment Works?

3 Explain what the reservoir at Foxpark is for.

4 Suppose you collected a glass full of rain water. What do you think would be in this water? Imagine that this rain water fell into Colliford Lake. What would happen to it as it made its way to a house in Penzance through the distribution network shown in picture 5?

Even after purification like this, the water contains dissolved substances. But these are harmless, so it doesn't matter if we drink them.

Supplying water in Cornwall

This is how water is distributed to homes in Cornwall.

Colliford lake is capable of supplying Cornwall with 24 million gallons of water every day. Water from the lake is released into rivers. It finishes up at Restormel Water Treatment Works. After treatment, water is pumped to a high level concrete service reservoir at Foxpark. This reservoir can hold 5 million gallons of water. From here the water supplies most of Cornwall.

The map in picture 5 shows the distribution network.

Picture 5 A map showing the distribution of water in Cornwall.

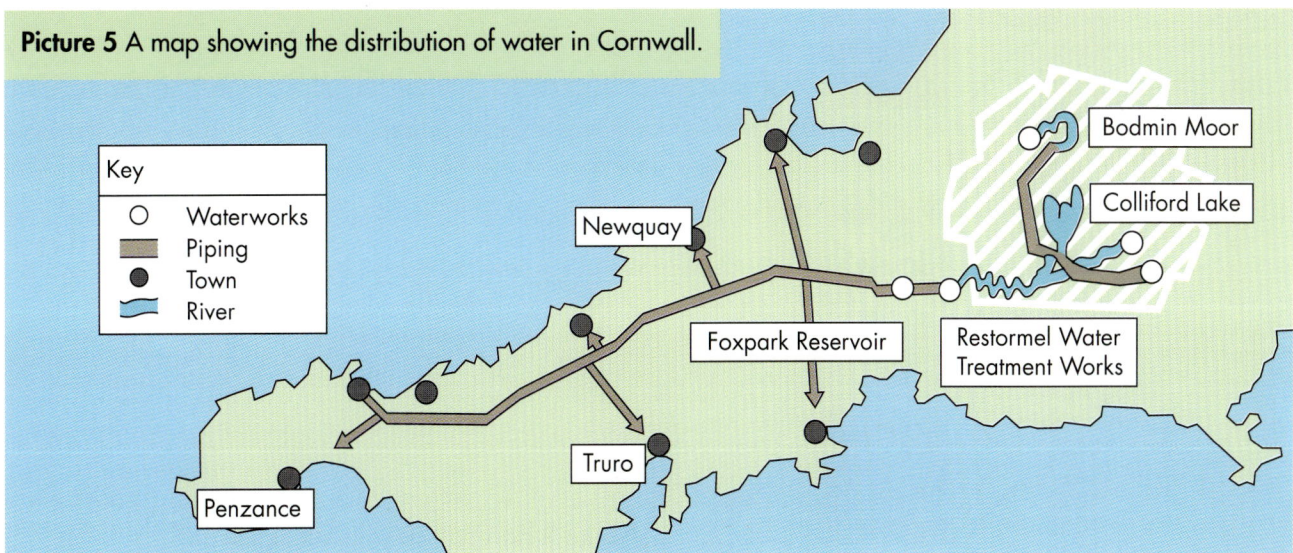

Key
○ Waterworks
— Piping
● Town
~ River

Bodmin Moor

Colliford Lake

Newquay

Foxpark Reservoir

Restormel Water Treatment Works

Truro

Penzance

4.2 Solids, liquids and gases

The states of matter

Water is usually a liquid. But it can also be a gas (steam) and a solid (ice). *Solid*, *liquid* and *gas* are called the three **states of matter**. (Matter is the name we give to all the different kinds of materials the World is made from.) All matter is made up of particles. How do these particles behave in solids, liquids and gases? Look at picture 1.

Liquid particles move around freely but are still attracted to each other.

Gas particles are fast moving and very spaced out.

Solid particles are packed tightly together and held by strong, attractive forces.

Picture 1

Changing state

What would happen to the particles in ice if we started to heat it up? Look at picture 2. In ice the particles are packed tightly together. If we heat the ice then the particles get more energy and start to move faster. At 0°C they have enough energy to break free. The ice turns to water.

If we continue to heat the water, the particles move faster still. At 100°C they become completely free and the water boils. It becomes a gas.

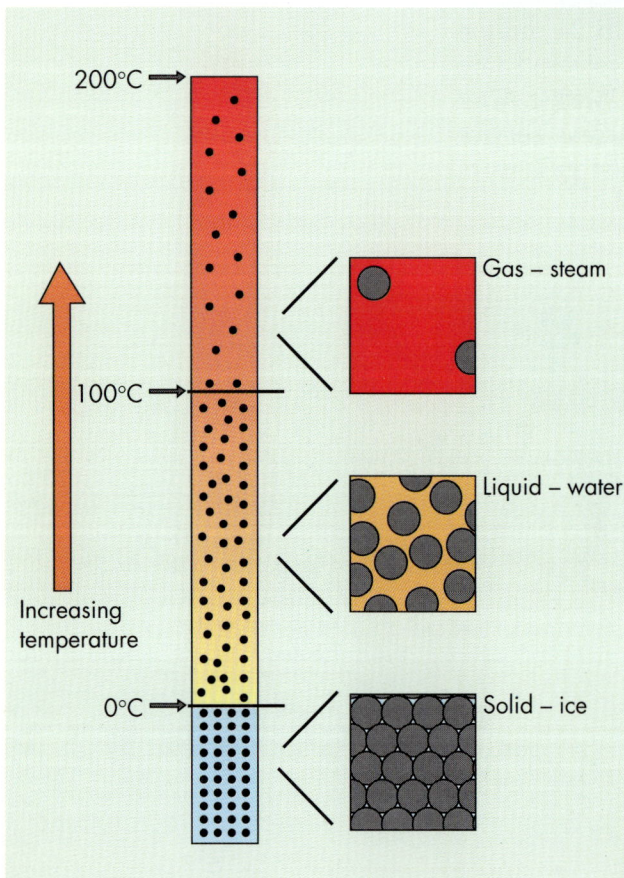

200°C

100°C

Increasing temperature

0°C

Gas – steam

Liquid – water

Solid – ice

Picture 2 How particles in solid, liquid and gas behave at different temperatures.

It's important to understand what particles are doing

Scientists around the World are investigating many new materials. They need to understand what the particles are doing in these materials.

'Kevlar' is a very strong material used to make bullet-proof vests. It has long, thin particles which pack closely together, side by side. This is what makes it so strong, yet flexible.

Along with new materials, new problems emerge. A plastic bottle discarded at the roadside will still be there 200 years later. Why? This is because the particles in the plastic cling together and will not easily spread out and disperse. Can scientists make new plastics that break down in sunlight? Only by understanding 'plastic particles' will scientists find an answer.

Picture 3 Materials called 'superconductors' promise faster computers and 300 mile an hour trains that are levitated from the ground.

Picture 4 Carrying a car engine is no problem when it is made out of plastic. Plastic engines could save petrol and help the environment.

Picture 5 shows the states of different substances at different temperatures. The line represents room temperature (25°C).

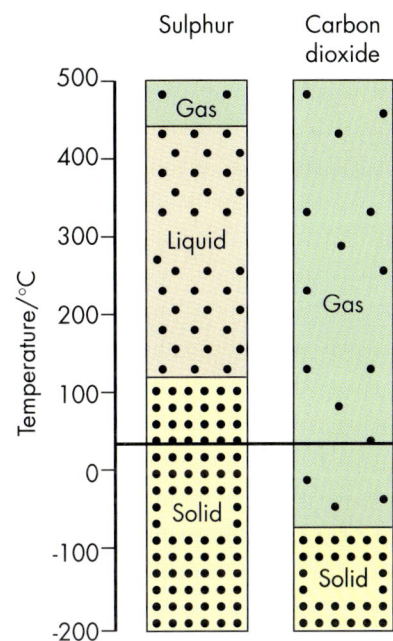

Picture 5

1 What are the states of sulphur and carbon dioxide at (a) room temperature? (b) −50°C? (c) 250°C?

2 What is unusual about the diagram representing carbon dioxide?

3 Copper is a metal that melts at 1083°C and boils at 2967°C. Draw a block diagram, similar to the ones in picture 5, to represent copper. Do it for a temperature range of 800°C to 2800°C.

4 Look at picture 2. Use the particle pictures to explain why solids are usually hard but liquids are not.

71

Picture 1

- Where does rain come from?
- How is it formed?

- Why does the level of water in a reservoir drop quite rapidly in hot weather?

- Sarah told Vipul that he could be drinking water that had at some time been flushed down the toilet. What do you think?

- Each of us uses about a swimming pool's worth of water every two years. Why do we never run out of water?

4.3 The water cycle

Do you know the answers to the questions in picture 1? The key to answering these questions is **nature's water cycle**.

Heat from the Sun causes water to **evaporate** from rivers, lakes and oceans. It turns to water vapour.

Look at the water cycle in picture 2. Like everything else, water is made up of tiny particles, far too small to see. We call these particles **molecules**. Notice how the water particles that evaporate from the sea do not take particles of dissolved substance with them. Can you see how nature is **purifying** the water in this way?

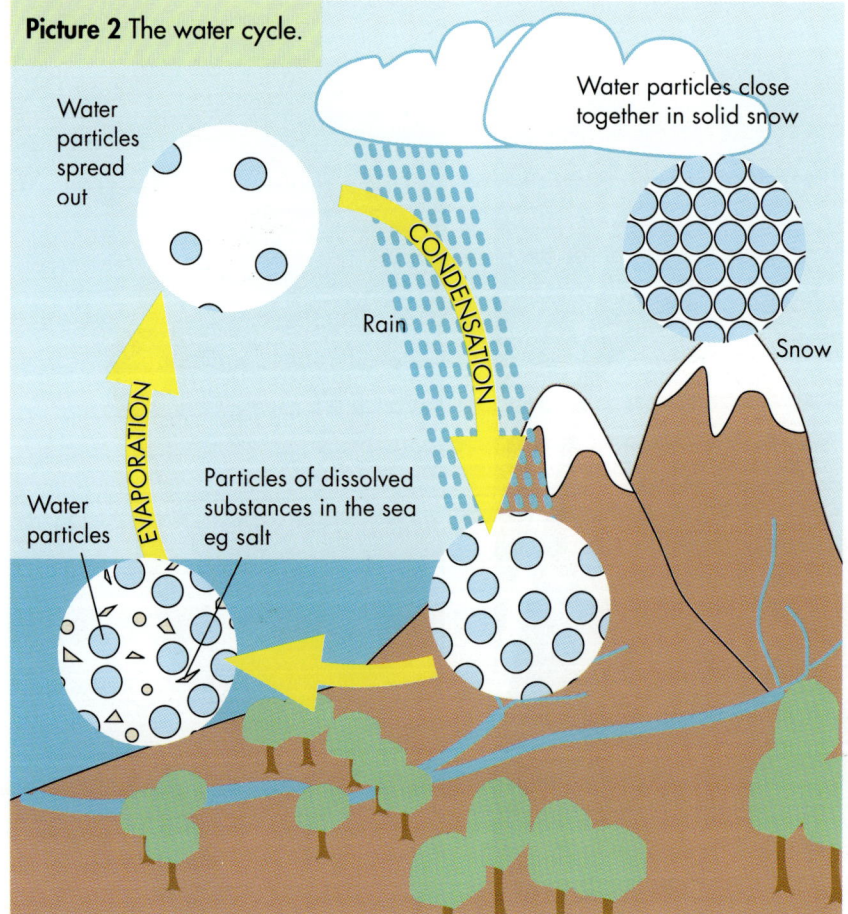

Picture 2 The water cycle.

The water vapour collects as clouds. As the clouds rise, the vapour cools down. It **condenses** as *droplets of water* – **rain**! So the water returns to Earth. It runs into streams and rivers – and eventually back to the sea. The water has gone round a cycle – the water cycle.

Storing water

The water that we use is stored in lakes and reservoirs. When it rains a lot, more water flows into them and they fill up.

In summer we tend to use more water for things like watering gardens. The hot weather also makes water evaporate more rapidly from the surface of a reservoir. If reservoir levels fall too far, then the Water Board need to make decisions to save water.

Picture 3 A dried up reservoir bed.

Picture 4 Water levels drop!

What happens to water after it has just rained?

Explain what you think would happen to the water in the different places shown in picture 5, if the weather changed in each of the ways as described by questions 1 to 4. Try to explain each of your answers. Think about what happens to the particles of water.

1 The day remained cold and windy.

2 The Sun came out and it was hot all day.

3 It was hot and windy all day.

4 It was cold and damp all day.

5 Rain water is mostly water that has evaporated from the sea. So why isn't rain salty?

6 What happens to the water cycle in very cold places?

Picture 5 10.00am:– It has been raining hard all night and has just stopped. The washing on the line was left out during the night.

Water on flat roof

Water on clothes

Water in barrel

Water on leaves

Water on grass

73

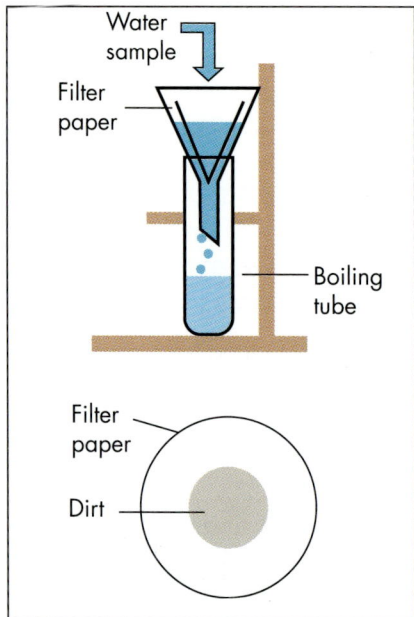

Picture 1 Apparatus needed to carry out a filtration.

4.4 Testing riverwater samples

Rivers pass through many different places. As they flow along, the water picks up many different substances. It may collect

- fertilisers from farmland
- bacteria from sewage works
- dissolved chemicals from industries.

How can we test to see if these substances are present in a sample of water?

Testing for dirt

What we call 'dirt' in dirty water is really tiny bits of solid, such as clay. We can see how much dirt is in a sample of river water using filtration. Picture 1 shows the method.

Testing the pH of water

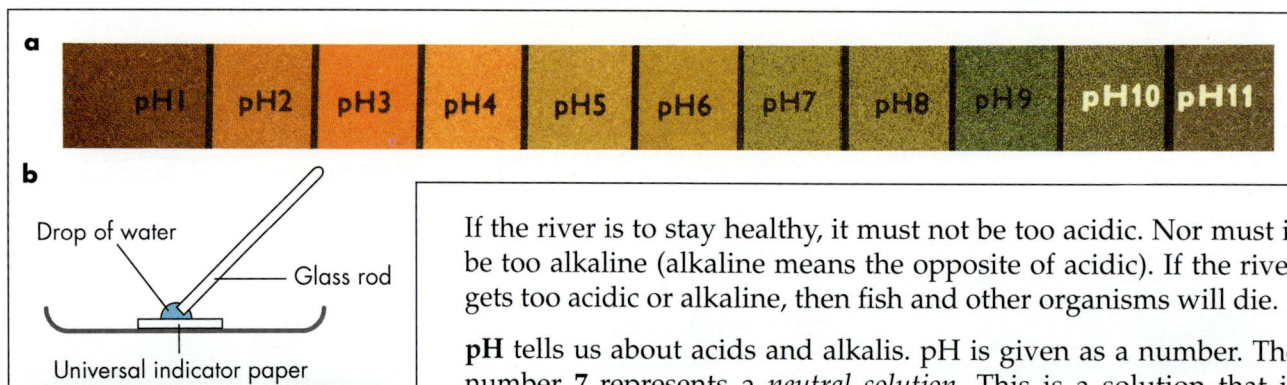

Picture 2 a The pH scale. **b** Testing the pH of water.

If the river is to stay healthy, it must not be too acidic. Nor must it be too alkaline (alkaline means the opposite of acidic). If the river gets too acidic or alkaline, then fish and other organisms will die.

pH tells us about acids and alkalis. pH is given as a number. The number **7** represents a *neutral solution*. This is a solution that is neither acidic nor alkaline. A number **less than 7** means that *acid* is present and the lower the number, the more acidic the solution is. Any number **above 7** means that *alkali* is present. The higher the number gets above 7, the more alkaline the solution is. Picture 2 shows how to test the pH of water.

Substances dissolved in water

Even after you have filtered a sample of water, there are still solids dissolved in it which you cannot see. You can see how much solid was dissolved if you boil away the water. Picture 3 shows how you do it.

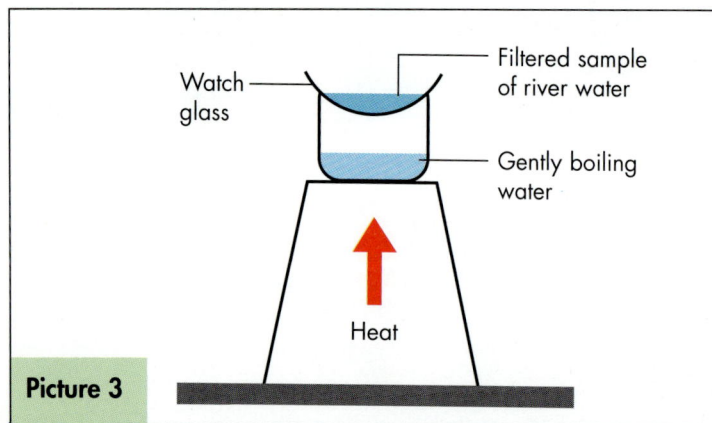

Picture 3

Testing for microbes

'**Microbes**' is the name we give to tiny organisms like bacteria that are too small to see. You can find the number of microbes in a water sample by growing them.

You can grow microbes in a dish, on a special jelly that feeds them. The dish is left in a warm place for a few days. Groups or **colonies** of microbes can then be seen. These microbes must be sealed in the dish and then destroyed, as some could be harmful to humans.

Water sample at site	A	B	C	D	E
Filter paper after filtration	◯	●	●	●	◯
Temperature/°C	6	8	11	18	7
Dissolved oxygen /parts per million	14	12	2	1	12
pH	7	7	6	6	7

Table 1

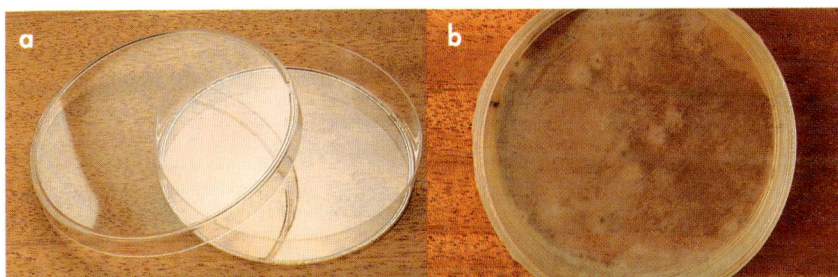

Picture 4 a Microbes are left to feed on the jelly. **b** After a few days in a warm place, colonies of microbes can be seen.

A riverwater problem

A scientist took samples of water from five sites along a river. Picture 5 is a map of the river. The scientist tested water samples A to E. The results of the tests are in table 1.

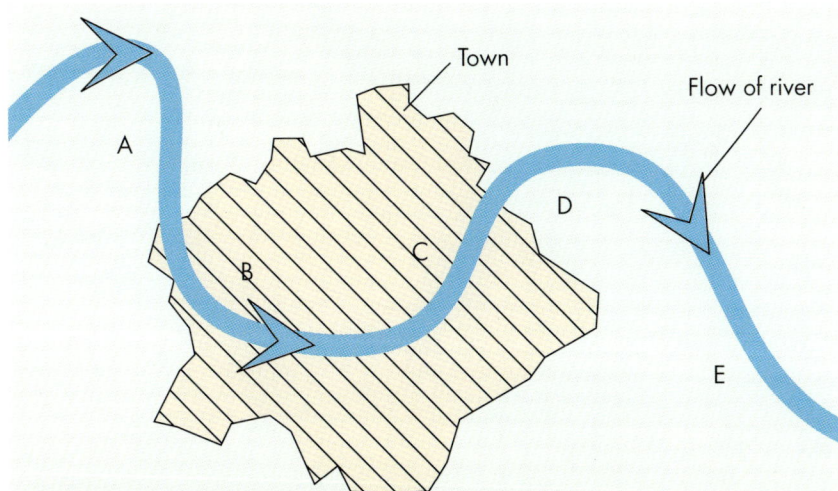

Picture 5 This map shows the five sites a scientist used to take water samples from a river.

Use table 1 to answer the following questions.

1 At which site was the water sample the dirtiest?

2 What do the pH readings tell you about the state of the water at the different sites?

3 In what way are the temperature of the water and the dissolved oxygen figures connected to each other?

4 What does your answer to question 3 mean for the fish in the river?

5 If a 'microbe count' was done at the different sites, at which site would you expect the count to be the biggest? Why?

Picture 1 All this damage due to air particles?

4.5 Winds

What is wind?

Air is invisible and most of the time we forget that it is there. Like all matter it is made up of particles. **Wind** is *moving air*. We can see the effects of moving air particles by watching leaves and washing on a windy day. We feel wind because air particles batter against our face.

Why do winds blow?

The battering of air particles causes air **pressure**. In some places air pressure is *high*. We call these places **anticyclones**. In other places pressure is *low*. They are **depressions**. Wind blows from high to low. Look at picture 2. Notice the words HIGH and LOW on this weather map.

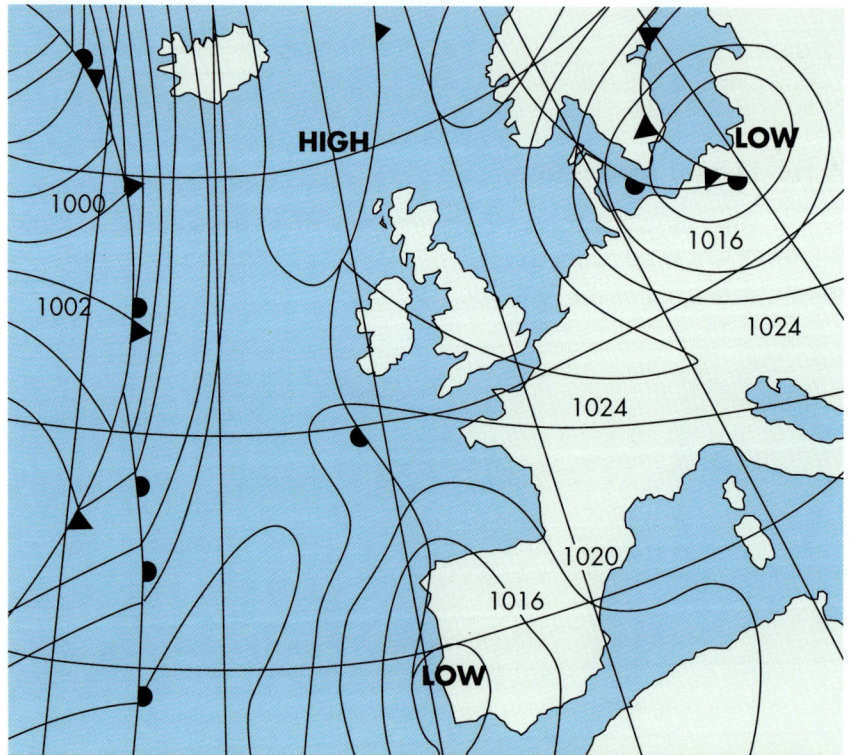

Picture 2 A weather map.

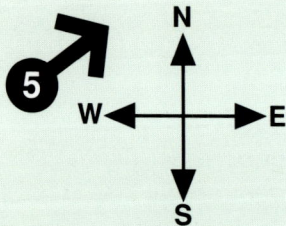

Picture 3 A wind speed symbol and compass bearing.

Wind has both speed and direction. Look at picture 3. The wind symbol gives the direction **from** which the wind blows and its speed in miles per hour.

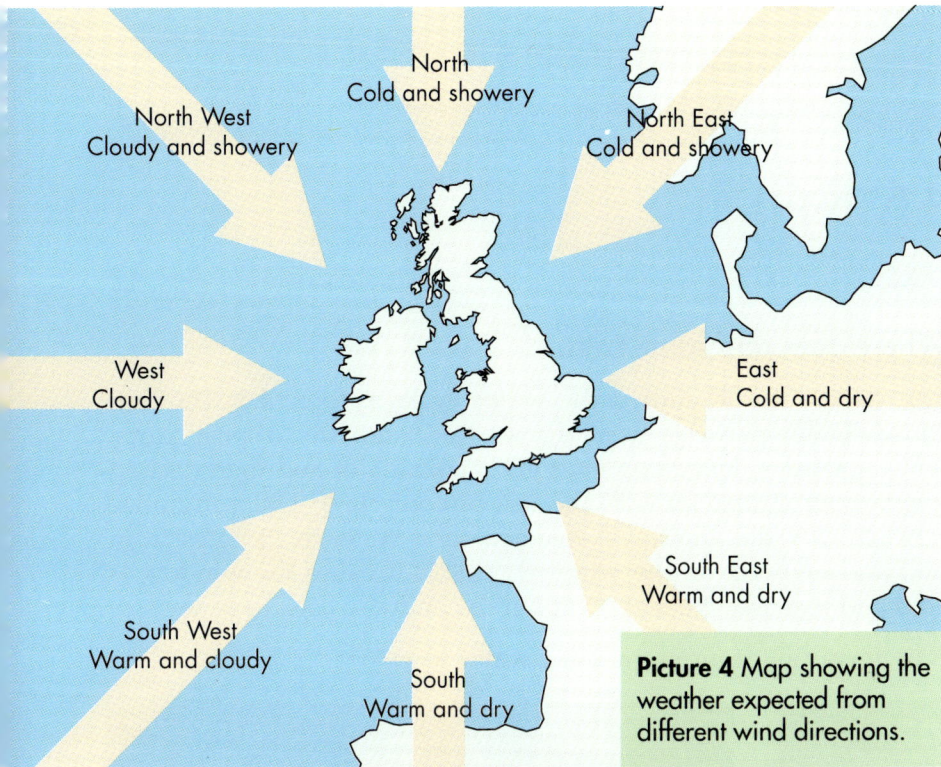

Picture 4 Map showing the weather expected from different wind directions.

Why is wind sometimes hot and sometimes cold?

Winds from the north bring cold air from the polar regions. Similarly, southerly winds tend to bring warm air from the equator. Also wind that crosses the sea is damp. Picture 4 shows this.

How do we measure wind speed?

A way of estimating wind speed is given by the **Beaufort scale** (table 1). Wind speed can be estimated by observing trees, flags, smoke etc.

Beaufort scale	Description	Observations	Average wind speed (miles per hour)
0	Calm	Calm, smoke rises vertically.	0
1	Light air	Slight smoke drift from chimneys.	2
2	Light breeze	Wind felt on face, leaves rustle.	5
3	Gentle breeze	Leaves and small twigs in constant motion, flags flutter.	10
4	Moderate breeze	Small branches are moved, dust and paper fly around.	15
5	Fresh breeze	Small trees begin to sway.	21
6	Strong breeze	Large branches in motion, umbrellas used with difficulty.	28
7	Near gale	Whole trees in motion.	35
8	Gale	Breaks twigs off trees.	42
9	Strong gale	Slight structural damage e.g. slates and chimney pots removed.	50
10	Storm	Considerable structural damage.	59
11	Violent storm	Widespread damage.	68
12	Hurricane	Widescale destruction	Greater than 73

Table 1 The Beaufort scale. (Beaufort numbers of 11 and 12 are rarely experienced.)

QUESTIONS

1 Look at the weather map in picture 4 showing the weather expected for the British Isles from different wind directions. Explain why

(a) a southerly wind is warm.
(b) a northerly wind is cold.
(c) a westerly wind is wet.
(d) an easterly wind is dry.

2 Describe fully the wind shown by the symbol in picture 3.

3 Try to suggest in your own words why a weather forecaster often gets the weather wrong.

4 Look at the pictures in picture 5. Compare them with the Beaufort scale in table 1. For each picture estimate the number on the scale and also the wind speed that the number represents.

Picture 5

5 Suggest descriptions for the Beaufort scale that could be used by sailors at sea. (For example, 0 on the scale might be described by 'Level sea, no waves, only ripples'.)

4.6 Rain

Where does rain come from?

You have already studied the water cycle in topic 4.3. The Sun causes water particles from the sea to evaporate. Air can carry water particles. Have you ever got soaking wet and then dashed inside your classroom with the rest of your class? Did you notice how quickly the windows 'steamed up'? Water evaporates from you and ends up on the window. This is because the window is cold and it causes the water vapour to condense back to water.

Rain forms in the air in the same way.

Picture 1 'All steamed up'.

Picture 2 A foggy day.

What are clouds?

Think what it is like on a foggy day. The air feels very wet. Fog is simply low cloud, consisting of droplets of water. When small droplets join together to form big drops, they fall as rain.

Clouds form when warm, damp air cools.

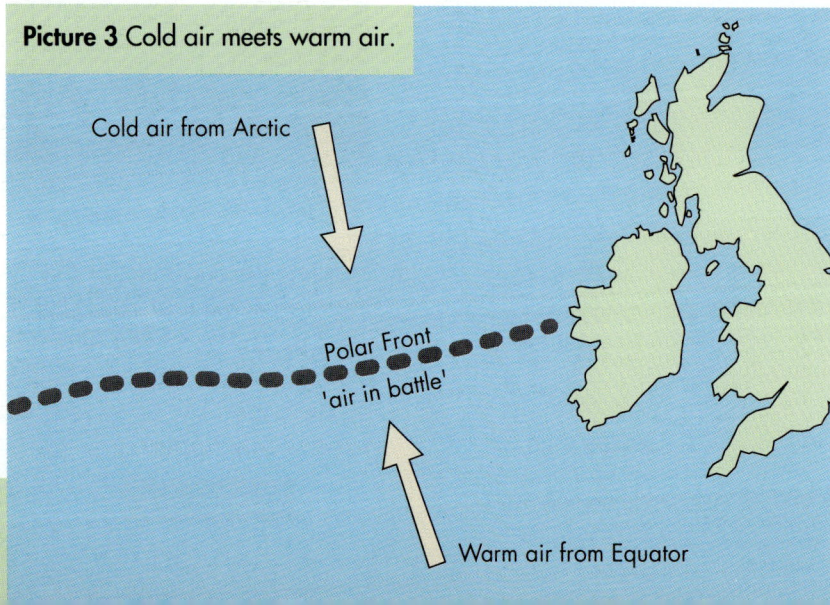

Picture 3 Cold air meets warm air.

Cold air from Arctic

Polar Front
'air in battle'

Warm air from Equator

What makes warm air cool?

There are many different climates in the World. The air at the Sahara Desert will be very hot, whereas at the North Pole it will be very cold. As air moves around, so warm air can meet cold air. **A weather front** *is a zone where winds carrying warm air and cold air are meeting or 'battling' together.*

A polar front occurs when cold air from the poles meets warmer air coming up from the equator. If the warm air is moving faster, it runs up the other side of the colder air, and pushes it away. This is called a **warm front**. But if the cold air is travelling faster, it burrows under the warmer air. This forms a **cold front**.

Will it rain or won't it?

How often do you watch the weather forecast to see if it's going to rain? A person who studies weather is called a **meteorologist**. How do meteorologists know that rain is on the way?

Radar is used to detect rain falling in distant places. The rainy area appears on a radar screen like a television picture. Look at picture 4 which shows a radar picture. Satellites in space can also be used to transmit pictures showing the position of cloud. Picture 5 was taken by a satellite.

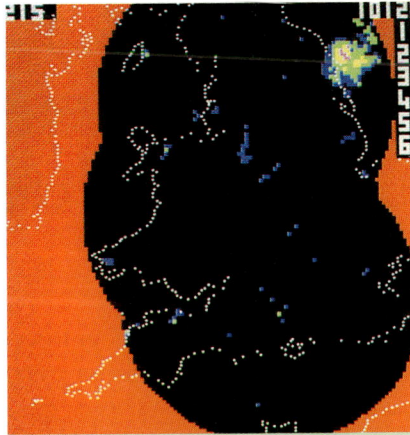

Picture 4 The light blue patches show rain falling.

QUESTIONS

1 What are clouds?

2 What is happening when clouds become darker and why does this usually mean that it will rain?

3 Fronts usually mean cloud and rain. Try to explain why.

4 Look at picture 4 again. Pretend that you are a weather forecaster. What would you say as you pointed to the picture?

5 In picture 5, what sort of weather would the Canary Islands be having? Explain your answer.

Picture 5 Swirls of low-level stratus clouds over the Canary Islands, as seen from space. (The Canary Islands are on the north-west coast of Africa.)

4.7 Our future climate?

Our planet is probably getting warmer. The 1980s saw the six warmest years in weather records. Burning fuels put polluting gases into the air. These gases then act like the glass in a greenhouse and keep the heat in. This is called the **greenhouse effect** and it leads to **global warming**. Carbon dioxide gas is the most important greenhouse gas, and millions of tonnes of it are produced by the petrol, gas and coal we burn every day.

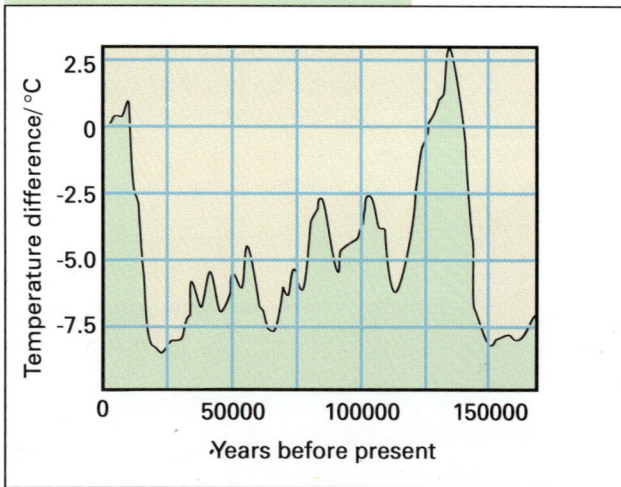

Picture 1 A graph showing how the Earth's average temperature has changed during the past 150,000 years.

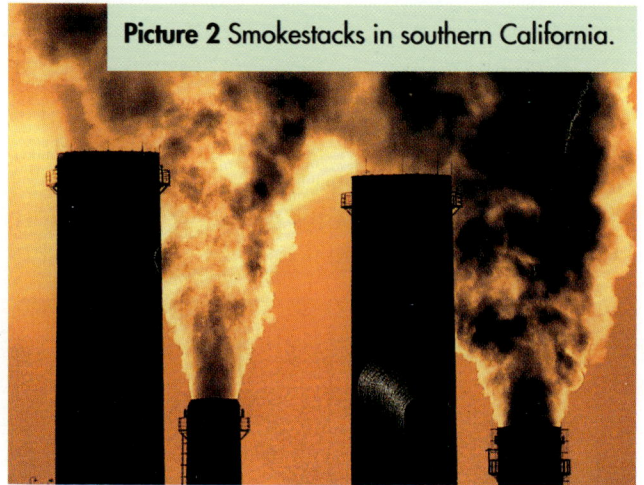

Picture 2 Smokestacks in southern California.

Would we benefit from a warmer World? Could we not grow more crops in a wider area? Perhaps we could in some areas, but what worries scientists most is the changes that could occur in the planet's weather patterns. Scientists make use of supercomputers, costing many millions of pounds each, in order to predict what the weather will be like in the next century. So what are the predictions?

What might happen?

Destructive droughts could strike more often and places that grow crops at the moment could turn semi-desert.

Forests could decline and change, and wildlife would have to find new habitats.

As ice on Greenland and Antarctica melts, the seas could creep higher onto the land. Large parts of low countries, such as Bangladesh – already swept by floods and typhoons – could be submerged. Cities like Miami, Venice and New York would need to be protected from the sea.

Picture 3 Burning fuels – power stations, cars and homes release carbon dioxide gas. Once in the air, the gas warms the air – the greenhouse effect.

Picture 4 A slight change in sea level could make the sea come further inland. This would threaten numerous wildlife species. For example, the sea could cover the home of the Florida panther.

But these are only predictions. Scientists know that the Earth is warming up, but they don't know for certain how this will affect our weather.

Some scientists think that we should act now to slow down the Earth's warming. They argue that the longer we wait the more difficult it might be to solve the problem.

The future may lie in the use of alternative ways of getting our energy that does not involve the use of fossil fuels. Solar and wind energy are examples.

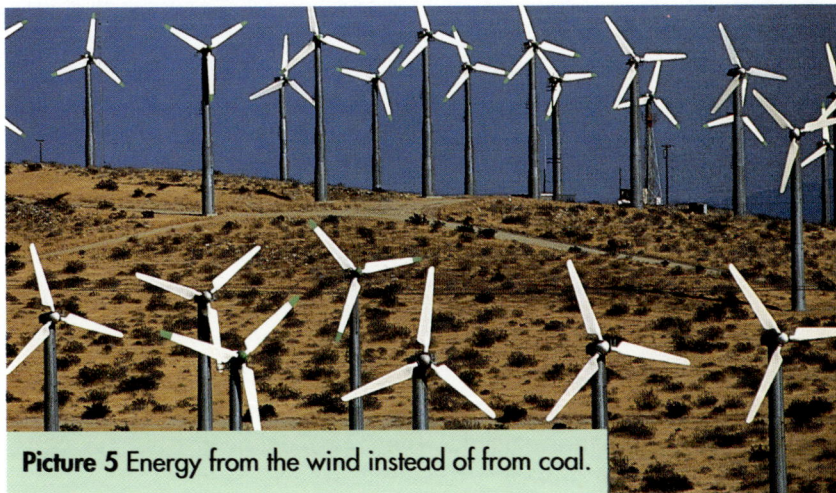

Picture 5 Energy from the wind instead of from coal.

QUESTIONS

1 Which gas is the major cause of global warming?

2 What do *you* think we should do to slow down global warming?

3 In what ways could global warming change future weather patterns?

4 Scientists are not sure how global warming will affect the Earth in the next century. They say that we should act now and not wait for proof. What do *you* think?

Life in a pond

What makes a healthy pond?

Water is essential for life. A pond is a **habitat** for many different species of animals and plants. The pond can change dramatically and make life very difficult for the plants and animals that live there. It can dry out in summer or become acidic due to rainfall. It can also become contaminated with sewage and other pollutants.

Picture 1 An unhealthy pond.

Fish in the pond need a good supply of the gas, **oxygen**. Plants in the water supply this gas and it also gets into the water from the air.

More about acidity

Rainfall has become more acidic over the years. This is because of pollutant gases from burning fuels. This rain makes ponds more acidic. Sometimes the acid can be **neutralised** by rocks, such as limestone on the bed of the pond.

A scale of numbers, called the pH scale, shows acidity (see topic 4.4). A pH of 7 is neutral. As the pH number drops below 7, so the water becomes more and more acidic. The more acidic it gets the more difficult it is for fish to survive.

The Woolmer Bog System – a collection of ponds

Picture 2 shows how a collection of ponds in Hampshire called the 'Woolmer Bog System' has changed over the years.

1 Describe how the ponds have deteriorated over the years.

2 Say why you think they have changed in this way.

3 Imagine that you are one of a group of school children who have decided to improve the Woolmer Ponds. Write down the sort of things that you would do. Think about the oxygen content of the water, the pH of the water and how to conserve the habitat of the plants and animals, especially the natterjack toad, that live in or around the pond.

Picture 2 The Woolmer Bog System from 1787 to 1986.

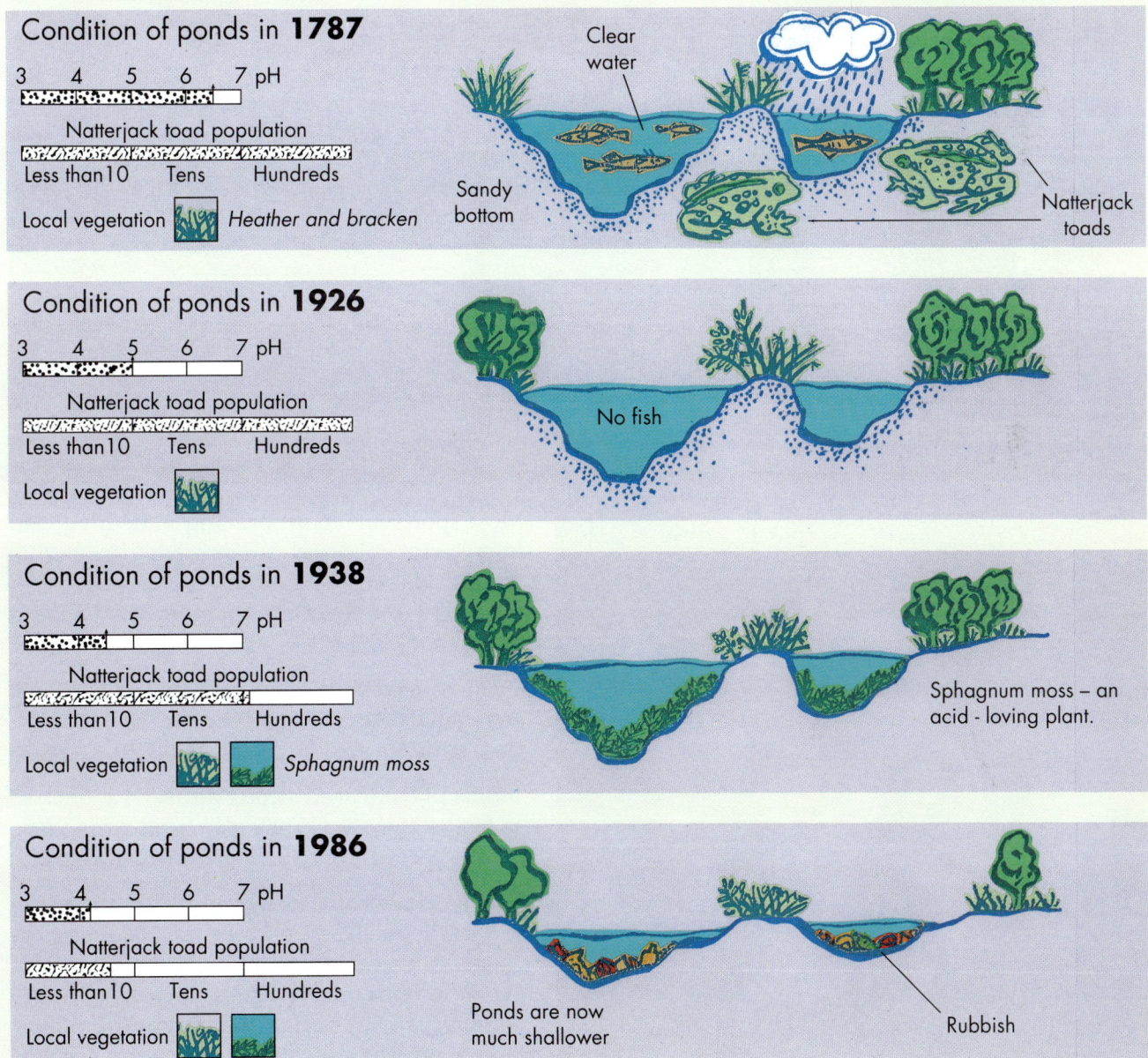

Condition of ponds in **1787**

3   4   5   6   7 pH

Natterjack toad population

Less than 10   Tens   Hundreds

Local vegetation   *Heather and bracken*

Clear water

Sandy bottom

Natterjack toads

Condition of ponds in **1926**

3   4   5   6   7 pH

Natterjack toad population

Less than 10   Tens   Hundreds

Local vegetation

No fish

Condition of ponds in **1938**

3   4   5   6   7 pH

Natterjack toad population

Less than 10   Tens   Hundreds

Local vegetation   *Sphagnum moss*

Sphagnum moss – an acid - loving plant.

Condition of ponds in **1986**

3   4   5   6   7 pH

Natterjack toad population

Less than 10   Tens   Hundreds

Local vegetation

Ponds are now much shallower

Rubbish

Topic 5 ■ GETTING GOING

5.1 Sport speeds

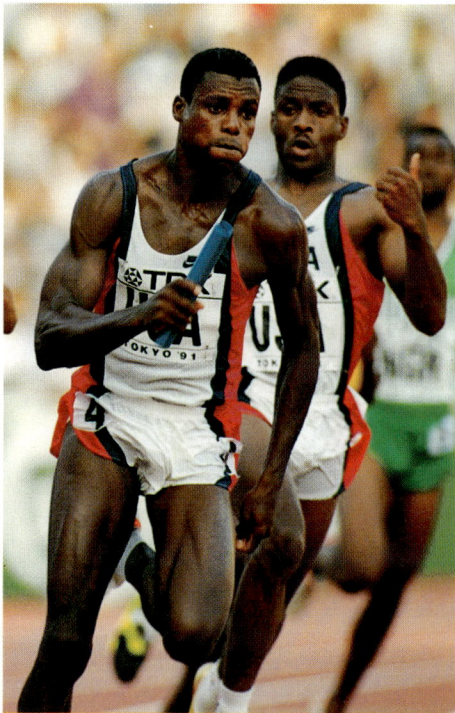

Picture 1 How fast does a sprinter run?

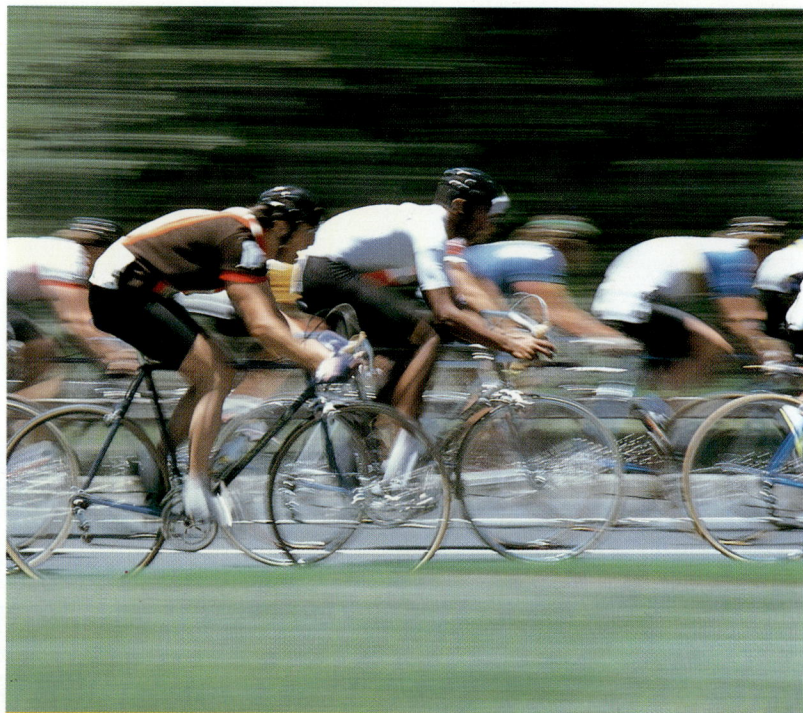

Picture 2 How fast do cyclists go?

Picture 3 How fast does the tennis ball go in a serve?

Most sports are about moving something fast. In a sprint race the runners have to go 100 metres as fast as possible. You can see from the muscles in their legs that they need a lot of strength to do this.

Cyclists need strong legs too, but their bodies are usually smaller and lighter than a top-class sprinter's.

Tennis players need strong arms to hit the ball as fast as they can. They also need strong legs because they have to run fast across the court.

The World record for running 100 metres is just less than 10 seconds. To run 100 metres in 10 seconds you would have to run 10 metres every second, on average. Can you see why? Another way of saying this is that the runner has an **average speed** of 10 metres per second.

Picture 4 The athlete has to cover 100 metres in 10 seconds. She could do this if she took just 1 second to run each 10-metre length.

Speed is *distance covered* divided by the *time taken* to cover that distance. In other words,

$$\text{speed} = \frac{\text{distance}}{\text{time}}$$

We measure speed in:
- metres per second (m/s)
- kilometres per hour (km/h)
- miles per hour (mph)

1 Can you think of any sports where speed is *not* important?

2 If you walk at 4 km an hour, how far should you get in 3 hours?

3 Use a calculator to find the average speed of
(a) an athlete who runs a 400 metre race in 80 seconds.
(b) a cyclist who travels 30 kilometres in 2 hours.
(c) a swimmer who swims 50 metres in 100 seconds.

4 Some cars can travel faster than others. Write down two things that you think decide how fast a car can go.

5 How far would you get if you cycled for 5 hours at a steady speed of 12 km/h?

Table 1

Speeds in sport	metres per second	km per hour
Average 12-year-old sprinter	5	18
World record sprinter	11	40
Average 12-year-old cyclist (over long distance)	5	18
Fastest animal (peregrine falcon, swooping)	97	350
Average speed of winner of the Tour de France race	10.5	37.8
Average speed of World record marathon runner	5.8	21
Speed of tennis ball service (at Wimbledon final)	44	160
Speed of cricket ball from fast bowler in Test Match	39	140
Speed of light	300 000 000	1 080 000 000

Picture 1 Spikes on a running shoe.

Picture 2 A tread pattern on a car tyre. It helps the car grip the road when it's wet.

5.2 Stopping and starting

Friction is important!

Picture 1 shows the spikes on a running shoe. Runners have to start running and pick up speed as quickly as they can. Their strong muscles wouldn't be much use if they slipped all over the place when they set off. Footballers wear boots with studs for the same reason. They have to stop and start very quickly, many times during a game.

Friction

Spikes and studs increase the **friction** between the shoe and the ground. Friction is the name of the force that 'grips' two surfaces together. When you start running your feet push back against the ground. The faster you try to go the harder you have to push. Your muscles are making as big a force as they can to get you going. This force has to act on the ground through the soles of your shoes.

If your feet don't grip the ground, all they do is slip backwards. You probably fall over. When your feet don't slip, your body moves forward. You do this so often, every day, that you probably don't realise how much science is going on!

Spikes aren't the only way to produce friction. For everyday movement leather or rubber soles will do. Both of these materials are non-slip on ordinary ground.

But if someone has polished the floor people can slip very easily. The polish makes the floor slippery. It has reduced the friction. Non-slip polish has to be used in schools to stop accidents. Loose mats or carpets can be just as dangerous.

Forces

When you walk, your feet actually push the whole Earth backwards! But the Earth is so big and massive that it doesn't move very far at all. If everybody in the World started running in the same direction at the same time, scientists could only just about measure the effect on the Earth.

But when you exert your force *you* move forward quite a lot. You are much smaller than the Earth, so the force from your leg muscles is enough to move you quite easily.

force pushing you along

force on ground

Picture 3 The forces exerted by a foot to move a body forward.

Stopping

You need a force to start something moving. But it also takes force to *stop* something. When you want to stop running, the friction force between your shoes and the ground stops you. Brakes produce the force to stop cars and bicycles. But brakes only stop the wheels turning. Unless the tyres get a good grip on the ground, the car or bike just carries on going. This is why there are so many more accidents on icy roads.

Picture 4 A bike brake.

Picture 5 Friction is used to stop a car. The shiny disc is connected to the wheel. The two pads grip the disc and the friction force acts on it to slow the wheel down.

QUESTIONS

1 Name two materials that have low friction (that are slippery) and another two that can make a lot of friction.

2 Imagine that the force of friction suddenly vanished. Describe two or three problems that this would cause. (Think about: getting up, dressing, having breakfast, going to school etc.)

3 What parts of a bike need
(*a*) very low friction?
(*b*) a lot of friction?

4 Name two substances we can use to cut down friction forces in a car, bike or tool.

5 (*a*) How does the brake block of a bicycle stop the wheel going round? (Look at picture 4 or a real bike.)
(*b*) Suppose you could buy a brake block that worked so well that the wheel stopped as soon as the brake was put on. Do you think it would be good idea to use a brake block like this? Give a reason for your answer.

5.3 Faster and faster

When something is going faster and faster it is **accelerating**. To make this happen, you need a force. When the driver of a car puts his or her foot down on the accelerator, the engine works harder and produces a larger force. The force is carried through to the wheels. The tyres push harder against the ground. The car **accelerates**.

Table 1

	CITROEN	FIESTA XR2i	ESCORT	ROVER
Top speed (kph)	167	184	166	204
Acceleration (0–100kph in seconds)	12.4	8.7	12.8	9.5
Mass (kg)	945	890	950	1367
Engine power (kW)	56	82	54	100

Picture 1 1 N acting on 1 kg of sugar makes it accelerate by 1 metre per second.

1 newton

Silver spoon

1 Kg

Picture 2 The gravity force acting on 1 kg of sugar.

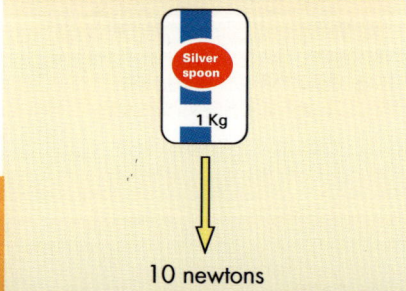

Silver spoon

1 Kg

10 newtons

Acceleration is a sure sign that there must be a force acting. We measure force in **newtons**. One newton isn't a very big force. It's the force you'd need to lift up a medium-sized apple. One newton is the force that can make a mass of 1 kg (say a bag of sugar) go faster by a metre per second every second (picture 1).

Compare this with the force of gravity on the bag of sugar. If you let the bag fall, it would increase its speed by ten times as much every second. This means that the 'gravity force' on the 1 kilogram bag of sugar must be 10 newtons.

The force of gravity acting on something is called its **weight**. Because it is a force, it is measured in newtons. But in everyday life we talk about something's 'weight' in kilograms or pounds. In fact, kilograms and pounds are a measure of its **mass**. There is more about this in topic 5.8.

What decides how well a car can accelerate?

An ordinary car can reach a speed of 100 km an hour in about 10 seconds. With a greater acceleration it could reach this speed in less time – say, in 5 seconds. How could you make it do this?

One way might be to give it a more powerful engine. This would produce a bigger force to accelerate it. Picture 3 shows a car specially designed to have a very large acceleration. You can see the large engine. This kind of car is designed for the sport of 'drag racing'.

Picture 3 A drag racing car.

But you can also see that it has very large wheels and tyres. A powerful engine is no good unless the forces it can produce actually get to act on the road. This is what the large tyres are for. Ordinary wheels and tyres would just slip.

Also, the car is made as light as possible. The heavier the car – the more **mass** it has – the harder it is to accelerate it. You wouldn't get much performance from a minibus powered by a minicar engine!

So the most important things that decide a car's acceleration are:

- the force it can get to act on the road
- how heavy the car is (its mass).

QUESTIONS

1 In what units do scientists measure
(a) force?
(b) weight?

2 Which could accelerate the most?
a A massive car with a small engine.
b A small car with a small engine.
c A small car with a large engine.

3 Good sprinters have much bigger leg muscles than good long distance runners. Why do you think this is?

4 Look at the data about cars in table 1 and answer the following questions.
(a)(i) Which car has the biggest engine?
(ii) Which is the heaviest car?
(iii) Which car has the biggest acceleration?
(b) Use the data to plot a graph of engine size (given in cubic centimetres) against the mass of the car (in kg). Use the axes shown in the graph below. Draw a line graph if you know how, but a barchart will do.

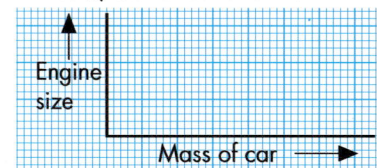

(c) Does the graph agree with the statement – 'Big cars have big engines'?
(d) Why should big cars need big engines?
(e) The data in table 1 is for the car plus a driver. What two measurements would change if the cars were loaded as much as possible with passengers and luggage?

5.4 Twin forces

What can make a force?

Muscles and engines aren't the only things that can make forces. There is the force of **gravity**, for example. There is more about gravity in topic 5.8.

Magnets attract each other with a **magnetic** force. If you rub a plastic pen with a cloth it will attract small pieces of paper with an **electric** force. When you stretch a rubber band you can feel a force pulling back on your hands – there is an **elastic** force in the band. Can you think of any other kinds of force?

Forces in pairs

Think of two magnets attracting each other. Have you noticed when you play with magnets that you can't tell which magnet is producing the force! In fact, both are. They attract each other with equal force. The first magnet pulls the second one just as strongly as the second one pulls the first (picture 1).

If you have experimented with static electricity you have probably found the same kind of effect. In fact, in every example you have come across in this topic so far, the force involved is really a *pair* of forces. This is true of forces produced by muscles and engines, as well as by magnets and electricity.

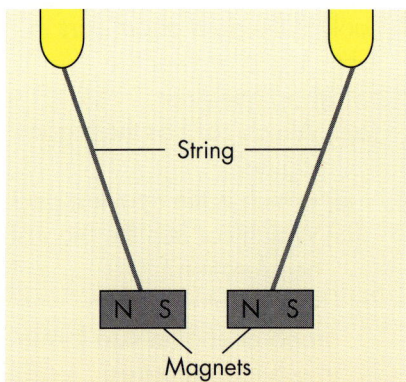

Picture 1 The magnets attract each other equally.

Picture 2 'Twin forces'

If you and a friend bang your heads together accidentally, both of you feel the pain! The force of the collision acts equally on both of you.

All forces come in pairs. The forces are always *equal* in size, and they always act in *opposite* directions. You might not believe this! But try to think of any force that just acts on one thing only.

Forces in springs

When you pull a piece of rubber cord it stretches. Also, you can feel the cord pulling back on your hands. If you let one end go it will move – and can be dangerous! Stretchy things like rubber and springs show quite clearly that forces come in pairs. (See picture 3.)

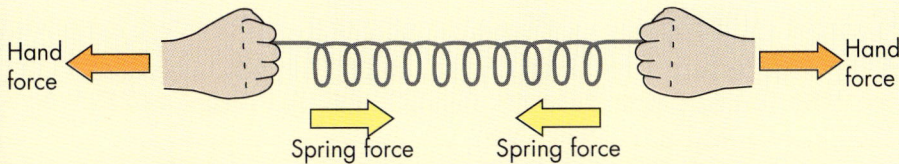

Picture 3 Forces come in pairs.

Any springy material is *elastic*. This means that a force can change its shape or make it longer. But it goes back to its ordinary shape when the force is taken away. Rubber is very good at this, which is why we talk about *elastic* bands. But steel is also elastic. We can use it to make springs.

Measuring forces

We often use a steel spring to help us measure forces.

Picture 4 shows the forces acting when we pull on a spring. The harder we pull, the longer the spring gets. We can mark off a scale to show how much the spring stretches. These markings also tell us how much force was exerted in newtons. We have made a newton-meter.

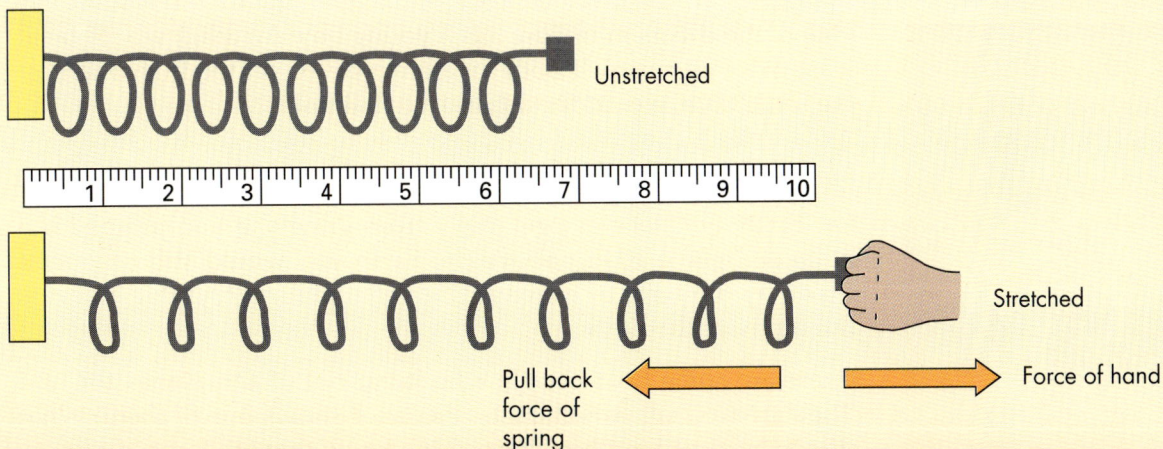

Picture 4 The two forces are equal. The spring stretches evenly as the force gets bigger.

1 Name as many kinds of force as you can think of.

2 Design an experiment to show that two magnets attract each other with equal-size forces.

3 (a) Name three things or materials that are elastic.
(b) Describe how you could test if one of the things you named is really elastic.

4 Name a material that isn't elastic. How would you prove it?

5 The force from the Earth's gravity pulls on the Moon and keeps it in orbit around the Earth. If forces always come in pairs, the Moon ought to somehow pull on the Earth. Can you think of any evidence that shows that there is a 'Moon force' acting on the Earth? (*Hint:* think of the seaside. You might answer this question better after tackling topic 5.8 *What is gravity*).

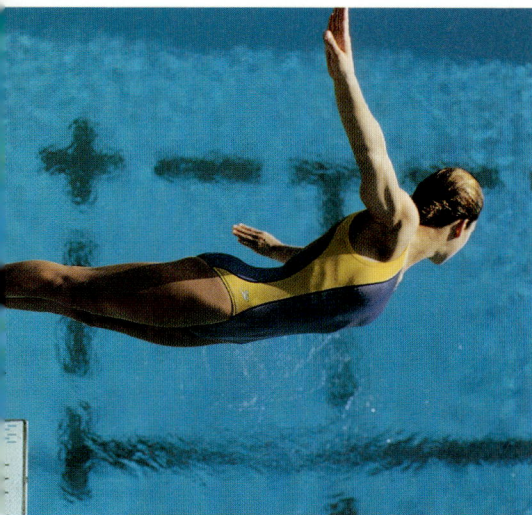

Picture 1 Taking a high dive.

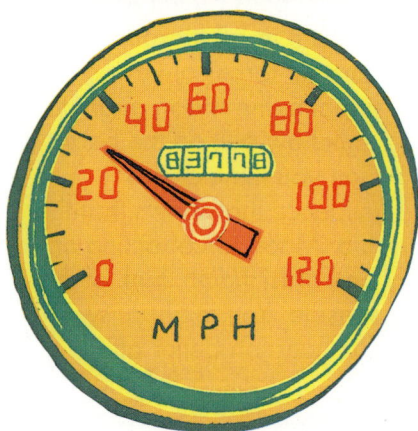

Picture 2 '14 metres per second'

Picture 4 Can you see the effect of an upward force?

5.5 Falling

Take a high dive!

Have you ever dived from the top board at a swimming pool? It takes a lot of courage!

The diver in picture 1 is falling. As she falls, she goes faster and faster. The force of gravity pulls her towards the centre of the Earth. She feels the air rushing past.

From a 10-metre board, the diver would hit the water at a speed of over 14 metres a second. This is faster than the speed limit for cars in towns (picture 2).

Picture 3 Which one would get to the water first?

One of the divers in picture 3 is a young boy. An adult would be at least twice as heavy. If both the divers dived off the high board at the same time, would the adult diver fall faster?

Free-fall parachuting

On Earth, we just can't get away from gravity. If you jumped out of an aeroplane 10 km above the Earth you would still be pulled down by the force of gravity. This force pulls everything towards the centre of the Earth.

There are some bold people who jump out of aeroplanes for fun! They are free-fall parachutists. Picture 4 shows one of them. What do you notice about her clothes? We know that the force of gravity is pulling her down. Can you see any evidence that there is another force acting on her?

When the parachutist jumps out of the aircraft she starts falling faster and faster. But remember what happens when you go faster and faster on a bicycle. You feel the air pushing back at you more and more. The same thing happens to the free-fall parachutist.

The force of the air is called **air resistance**. It is a kind of friction force that slows you down. The faster you go, the bigger this force gets. After a while the falling parachutist can't go any faster. At this speed her falling body has enough air resistance pushing against it to balance the force of gravity exactly.

With a normal adult, this happens when the body is travelling at about 130 km per hour. This is called its **terminal velocity**. Of course, before the parachutist hits the ground she's opened her parachute!

The parachute slows her down a lot (picture 5). It does it by making the force of air resistance very much greater. The body slows down to about 10 or 15 km an hour. This is a much safer speed – but it can still break a leg! You need the right safety clothing and good training to avoid harming yourself.

Picture 5

Picture 6

QUESTIONS

1 What is the name of the force that pulls parachutists downwards?

2 How would the movement of a parachutist change if there was a strong wind blowing sideways?

3 Copy picture 6 and draw arrows on it to show the direction of the force of gravity acting on each object.

4 A parachutist is falling at a steady speed in still air. Does this mean that there are no forces acting on him or her? Explain your answer.

5 (a) Explain clearly why if you jumped out of an aeroplane
    (i) you would first fall faster and faster,
    (ii) then reach a steady speed.
  (b) Explain how a parachute would make this steady speed a lot smaller.

Picture 1 A mountain bike racer.

Picture 2 Having fun at a playground, safely.

5.6 Crashes and bangs

Young people enjoy exciting sports and games. But they do run risks. They fall off things and bump into things. Accidents will happen.

Bones are easy to break. The most dangerous or painful places are the head, the elbows and the knees. The young bike rider is protected by a crash helmet, elbow pads and knee pads.

We can't expect young children to wear all this gear just to use a climbing frame! But they do need protection. The floor below the climbing frame in picture 2 is made of special material. It is a lot softer than the concrete in the rest of the playground.

Forces and safety

Bones are broken by forces – like the force of a crash or collision. The faster you go, the bigger the force you can produce. So one way of not getting hurt is to move about very slowly! This would make life very boring.

But another way is to stop slowly. This is what brakes are for. But what if you do crash into something? You are bound to stop suddenly. But the more time you take to stop the better. *The longer you take to stop, the smaller the force you need.* (See picture 3.)

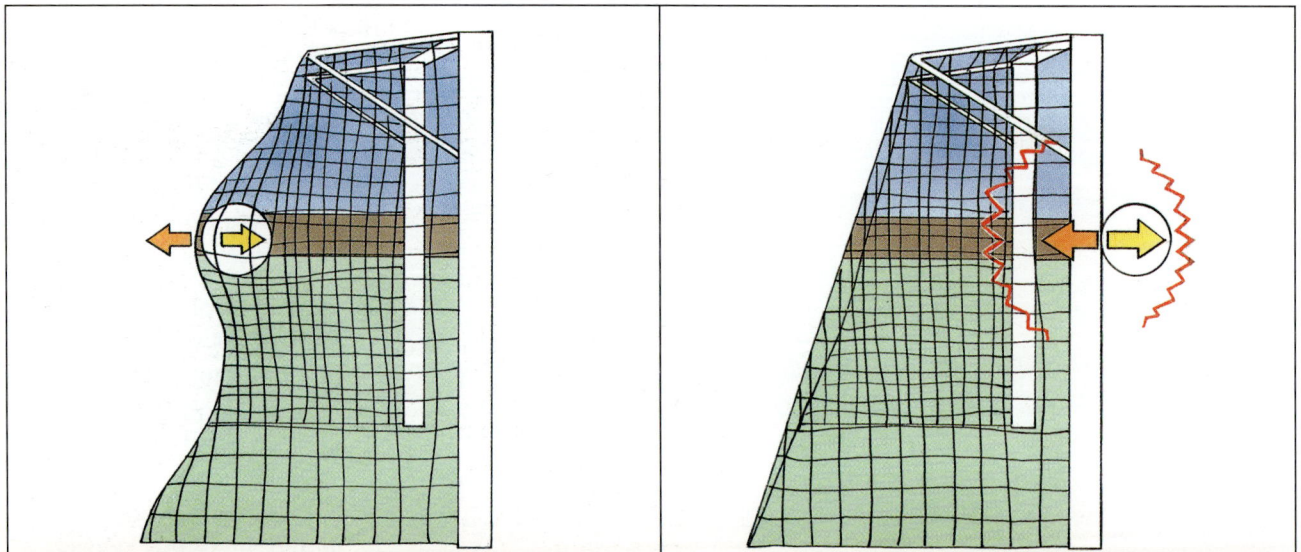

Picture 3 a Not much force acts when the ball is stopped slowly by the goal net.

b But a large force is produced when the ball hits the goal post and is stopped very quickly.

This idea is used in the design of the special playground floor. It squashes a little when a child falls on to it. This means that a falling child takes longer to come to a stop. The force acting on him is less and he is less likely to break a bone (picture 4).

Picture 4 The playground floor gives just enough to cut down the risk of serious injury. The body is stopped by a smaller force acting for a longer time.

Crash hats are designed so that they give a little. They also spread the force over a bigger area, so the effect on any one part of the head is less.

Knee and *elbow pads* spread the force of a fall over a bigger area. But they also protect the skin from cuts and nasty grazes.

Picture 5 shows men dressed in the gear needed to play American football. In this game, large men run very fast and have to crash into each other at high speed. This clothing is designed to do two things:

● make the collisions take longer to happen, so the forces produced are smaller;
● spread these forces out over a bigger area, so they don't act on just one small part of the body.

Picture 5 One American footballer tackles another.

QUESTIONS

1 Do you play any game or sport in which you might be injured? If so, say what it is and describe what safety precautions you take against being injured.

2 High jumpers and pole vaulters have to jump as high as they can. How are they protected from injury as they come down again?

3 Why is it more dangerous to fall onto concrete than onto a grassy field?

4 In a circus, trapeze artists use *safety nets*. Draw a picture showing what happens when somebody falls into one of these nets. Explain how it protects the trapeze artist from injury.

5 It takes less force to stop a moving object if you take a longer time to stop it. Design an experiment to see if this statement is true.
Hints: You can measure a force with a spring balance or a force meter. You could use a net or rubber bands, to help stop a falling object more slowly. You could use a block of wood as the object. Check to make sure that your test is fair.

5.7 Safety and cars

Picture 1 A car crash in progress.

Picture 1 shows what happens in a car crash. It took just one-fifth of a second to stop the car. It was travelling at 30 mph (50 km per hour).

The car was designed to stop as slowly as possible, even in a crash. This was done by having a *crumple zone* at the front end, where the engine is. The front part of the car is made weak enough to crumple up gradually. The car takes longer to stop than if it was made stronger. So the force on the car is less than it might be if it was solid.

How do seat belts help to save lives?

The driver is held by a seat belt. This makes her stop in the same time as the car does. In fact the belt stretches a little, so she stops even more slowly than the car does. The force to stop her is produced by the seat belt. This force is enough to make bruises, but she should not be hurt too much.

The passenger is a young girl. She was sitting in what her mother thought was the safest place – the back seat. The front seat seems to be the most dangerous place to be if there is an accident.

But the girl wasn't wearing a seat belt. Even though she was sitting in the back seat of the car she wasn't safe.

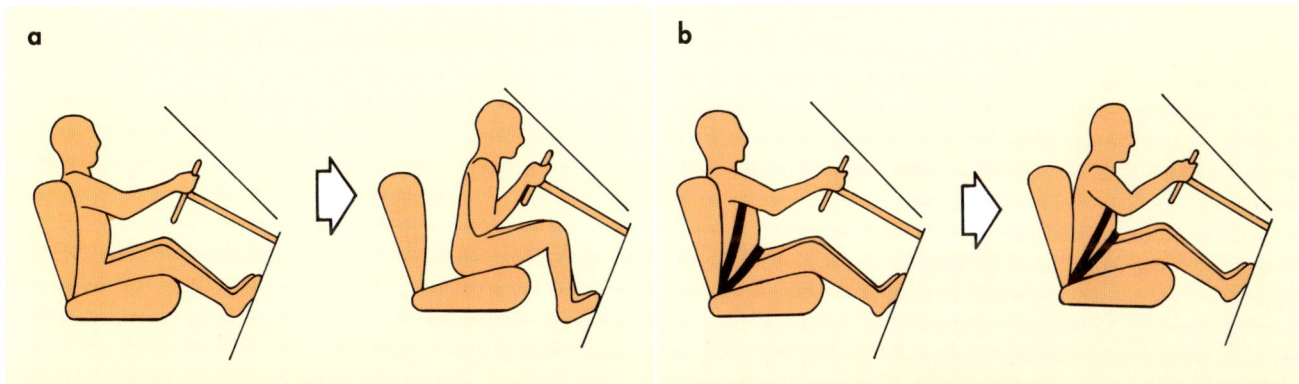

Picture 2 a If no seat belt is worn, the person keeps moving forward and hits the windscreen – hard!
b With a seat belt the person stays with the seat. The belt is designed to give a little, so that its force on the body acts for a longer time.

She doesn't stop when the car stops. She carries on moving. There is no force acting on her to make her stop.

But then she hits the windscreen. If the windscreen is a modern one it is made of safety glass. It will break. The girl's face will be cut by the broken pieces as she flies through it. If she is lucky she will survive.

If the windscreen doesn't break, but just *bends*, the child is stopped very very quickly. This needs a large force. The child's head could be crushed, and she might die.

All new cars must have rear seat belts fitted. Anybody sitting in the rear seat must wear a seat belt. Make sure that you obey this law.

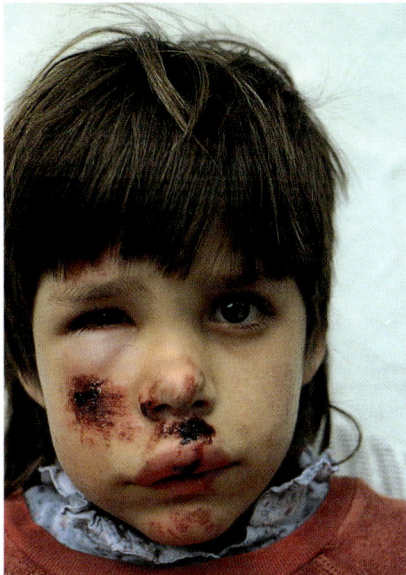

Picture 3 This little girl was lucky. The windscreen broke.

Picture 4 A 30 mph speed limit sign.

QUESTIONS

1 Copy out the sentences below and fill in the missing words.
(a) In a crash, a car stops quickly, and a large _____ acts on it.
(b) Brakes make a car stop _____, so less _____ is needed.

2 Why must people wear seat belts, even when they are in the back seat of a car?

3 Suggest two reasons why there are speed limits for cars in towns and villages.

4 What is the *crumple zone* of a car? How does it help save lives in an accident?

5 Modern windscreens are made of special safety glass. It is strong but will break more easily than the older toughened glass that was used before. Why is it better for the windscreen to break in an accident, and not just bend a little?

Picture 1 A waterfall.

Picture 2 An astronaut 'space walking'.

Picture 3 Isaac Newton.

5.8 What is gravity?

The water in the waterfall is falling towards the centre of the Earth. It is pulled down by a force that we call the force of **gravity**. What about the astronaut? He is about 200 km above the surface of the Earth. Is he affected by gravity?

Apples – and the Moon

Most of our ideas about gravity come from one of the most famous scientists of all time. His name was Isaac Newton. He lived about 300 years ago (1642 to 1727). Put simply, what Newton said was this.

'Things feel heavy because of the force of gravity due to the Earth. But every object that exists can produce this force of gravity, and it acts on every other object.'

The Earth pulls down at an apple on a tree. When the apple is ripe it falls. But the apple also pulls back on the Earth! The force is the same. But the apple is smaller and easier to move, so it falls.

In fact, Newton thought up his theory of gravity while sitting in an orchard at home. He wondered if the force pulling on an apple was the same kind of force that kept the Moon going around the Earth.

How strong is gravity?

The force of gravity is pretty weak, compared with a force like magnetism. You exert a gravity force on the person sitting next to you. But the force is far too small for you to notice it. You don't stick together like two magnets!

But the gravity effect of a very large object, like the Earth, is very large. It produces a force of about 10 newtons on every kilogram of matter on Earth. This force is called the **weight** of the object. If you have a mass of 50 kilograms, then your weight is about 500 newtons.

Mass was another idea of Newton's. He said that mass is how much material an object has. This is the same wherever it is. But its weight could change, because the weight depends on the strength of your local gravity. You would still be you even on the Moon – but there you would only weigh about 80 newtons. This is because the Moon is a much smaller object than the Earth. So its gravity is not as strong.

The long arm of gravity

The force of gravity can act over any distance. But the force gets weaker with distance. The force of gravity from the Earth even

Picture 4 Earth's gravity acts as far as the Moon, and even further. But it gets weaker with distance.

reaches as far as the Moon. It holds it in its orbit around the Earth. Newton was able to work out the time the Moon should take to travel once around the Earth. It was exactly the same as the time measured by astronomers. This proved to Newton that his ideas were correct.

The astronaut in picture 2 is also orbiting the Earth. He too is attracted by the Earth's gravity force, and it is this force that keeps him in orbit. In the same way, the Earth and the planets of the Solar System are kept in orbit around the Sun by the huge gravity forces that the Sun can produce. Newton worked out his theories when he was a young man of 23 in 1665. The most spectacular proof of his theories came when astronomers used them to predict that a planet existed, deep in space, that no one had ever seen. In 1846 it was found and named Neptune.

QUESTIONS

1 Picture 5 shows some apples on two trees. One is in Australia, one in Britain. Which way would apples fall off the tree?

Picture 5

2 Draw a picture of the Moon and the Earth in space. There is a gravity force between them. Mark on it which way the force of gravity pulls on
(a) the Moon.
(b) the Earth.

3 Does the force of gravity act on the astronaut in picture 2? Give a reason for your answer.

4 Table 1 shows the masses of the planets in the Solar System, compared with the mass of the Earth.
(a) On which planet would you weigh most?
(b) On which planet would you weigh least?
(c) All the planets move in orbits around the Sun. It needs a force to keep something moving in a circle. (Think of whirling a conker around on a string.) What force keeps the planets in orbit?

Table 1									
Planet	Mercury	Venus	Earth	Mars	Jupiter	Saturn	Uranus	Neptune	Pluto
Mass (relative to Earth)	0.05	0.81	1	0.11	318	95	14.5	17.5	0.003

5.9 Galileo, Newton and gravity

Picture 1 A busy Italian street scene in the 17th century.

Picture 2 During the 17th century, a large number of scientific experiments were carried out. Isaac Newton experimented to investigate the spectrum of colours we get from a rainbow or a prism.

I MUST BE RIGHT. I'VE GOT MORE BOOKS THAN YOU!

AH! BUT MY BOOKS ARE OLDER THAN YOURS

Picture 3

People say that modern science began over 300 years ago, in the 17th century. Two of the most famous scientists of all time lived then. They both discovered many new things, and came up with new theories to explain them.

One was Italian. His name was Galileo Galilei. He was born in 1564 and died in 1642. The other was English. His name was Isaac Newton. He was born in the year that Galileo died, and lived until 1727.

What made these scientists modern wasn't just that they had the 'right' ideas. In fact, as with all scientists, sometimes they were right and sometimes they were wrong. *What was new was that they did experiments to check their ideas.*

If the results showed that the theories were wrong – then they changed the theories. Up until then many scientists just argued about the theories, and tried to prove them by quoting from ancient books that might have been written thousands of years before.

The old theories about why things fall used two ideas – **gravity** and **levity**. Things that fell, like stones off cliffs and apples off trees, had gravity. But some things went up – like flames and smoke. People believed they must have the opposite – something called levity. Heavy things must have more gravity than light things. So heavy things must fall faster than light things. This theory was 2000 years old – so it must be right!

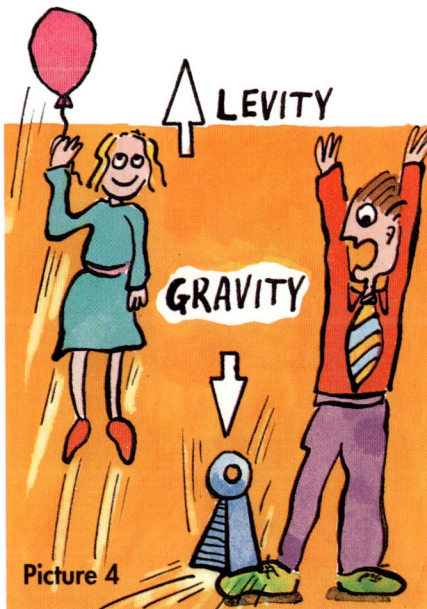

Picture 4

LEVITY

GRAVITY

But Galileo thought that it was wrong. 'All things ought to fall at the same rate,' he said. 'Why not do an experiment to find out?' Galileo tested this theory by rolling steel balls down a slope. He thought a better proof would be to drop heavy and light cannon balls from the Leaning Tower of Pisa, but never got around to doing it.

Galileo's experiments proved that heavier objects didn't actually fall faster than lighter ones. In fact all things fall at the same rate, and he measured this. We now call it the **acceleration of free fall.**

Galileo couldn't explain why this was. But Isaac Newton produced a full theory of gravity to explain it. (See topic 5.8.) Newton's theories became very important. They did more than explain how and why things fell on Earth. Newton proved that the force of gravity reached from Earth as far as the Moon. It explained the tides of the sea, which are caused by the forces of gravity from the Moon and the Sun. It explains that the Sun's gravity force keeps the planets of the Solar System in their orbits.

Newton's theories allowed sailors to work out where they were, when they were at sea. This helped them to make accurate charts, and to discover new lands, like Australia and New Zealand, and the new islands in the Pacific Ocean. Newton's Laws are still used today. For example, they are used to help get satellites into orbit, and control them when they get there.

Picture 5 Newton's theories helped the Captain navigate his ship and discover new land.

QUESTIONS

1 The old scientists used the ideas of gravity and levity. What is the difference between gravity and levity?

2 Name three things that the old scientists would say had gravity, and three that must have levity.

3 Give two useful applications of Newton's theories.

4 A steel ball will fall to the ground a lot faster than a feather. Does this contradict Galileo's idea that all things are supposed to fall at the same rate? Explain your answer.

5 If gravity pulls everything on Earth down, why
   (a) do bubbles rise in water?
   (b) does smoke rise?
   (c) can an aeroplane fly?

6 The old theory about gravity and levity was wrong. But it explained quite a lot of everyday things, so it wasn't a bad theory. Describe any other scientific theory you know about that we now think is wrong. Do you think it was a good theory, in its day? Give your reasons.

Designing

Forces act on objects to speed them up, slow them down or change their shape. Use what you have learned about forces and materials to design a solution for the following.

Choose any three tasks. Make a clear drawing of your solution. Label your drawing to explain the main points of your design.

A Design a car with a low drag factor.

B Design a tent that can stay up in a strong wind blowing from any direction.

C Design an egg-carrier for mountain climbers (who might drop things now and again).

D Design a wheeled vehicle that can travel over rough, steep ground which has large rocks up to 0.5 metres tall.

E Design a baby suit for a baby who is just learning to walk and falls over a lot.

Topic 6 ■ LIGHT AND SOUND

6.1 Thunder and lightning

When lightning strikes it makes a huge bang. Usually, however, we don't hear the thunder until some time after we have seen the lightning. The light and sound are both released at the same time, but the sound reaches us after the light. This tells us that sound must travel more slowly than light.

Picture 1 For every three seconds you count between seeing the lightning and hearing the thunder, you can say that the lightning struck one kilometre away.

Picture 2 The runners are close to the pistol. They start when they hear the bang. If you were further away you would hear the bang after the race started.

You don't notice this difference if someone is speaking to you. You see them say the words at the same time as you hear them. This is because the sound doesn't have to get very far. You only notice a delay for sound reaching you over longer distances. You may have found this at the running track when the starter fires his pistol. You always hear the shot after you have seen the smoke from the gun.

How fast is sound?

Suppose you were 100 metres from the starting pistol. There would be a delay of about a third of a second before you *heard* the bang. If you were 300 metres away, the delay would be nearly a whole second. Sound travels about 340 metres in one second. We say that the **speed of sound** is 340 metres per second.

You can use the speed of sound to find out how far away a lightning strike is. Start counting when you see the flash and stop when you hear the thunder. For every second that you counted, you can reckon that the sound has had to travel 340 metres. If you count to three seconds it has travelled about 1020 metres – or just over a kilometre.

450 — 450 m/s: Not many things travel faster than the speed of sound. **Supersonic** aeroplanes do. If an aeroplane travels at the speed of sound, we call its speed **Mach 1**. Some aeroplanes travel at **Mach 2** – twice the speed of sound.

380 — 380 m/s: A bullet travels faster than sound. This means that if someone shot at you (let's hope no one ever does!), you would feel the bullet before you heard the bang.

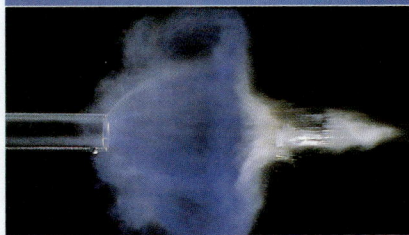

340 — 340 m/s: The speed of sound is about 340 m/s. It can vary slightly depending on weather conditions.

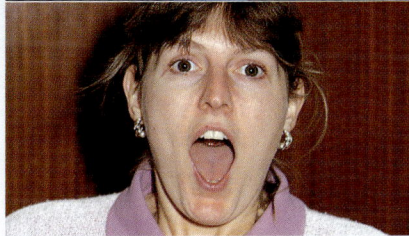

QUESTIONS

1 Give two differences between sound and light.

2 How do people communicate using
(a) sounds?
(b) light?

3 You see a lightning strike and start counting. You count to six before hearing the thunder. How far away did the lightning strike?

4 If someone shot at you, would you see the flash of the gun before you felt the bullet? Explain your answer.

5 The people timing a 100 m race stand at the finish, so that they can stop their clocks when the runners cross the line. They are told **not** to start their clocks when they *hear* the pistol shot.
(a) What is wrong with starting the clock when they hear the bang?
(b) When *do* they start the clock?

How fast is light?

So far we have assumed that the light reaches us the instant that the lightning struck. This is not true. Light does not reach you straight away, though the time it takes for light to reach you is very short.

The **speed of light** is 300 million metres per second. In one second, light would travel eight complete laps of the Earth. The light from the Sun has taken eight minutes to reach us.

To put the speed of light on the scale of speeds, the book would need to be 200 km tall – or the distance from London to Birmingham!

How else are light and sound different?

The Sun is a huge nuclear reactor out in space. It is making a lot of noise and a lot of light. If we put big microphones in space, would we be able to hear the Sun? We wouldn't because *sound* needs something to carry it and there is no air in space. It is a huge vacuum, so sounds from the Sun doesn't reach us. However, we can *see* the Sun; so its light must have travelled through space. Light *can* travel through a vacuum but sound cannot.

100 — 100 m/s: Sound travels 3.4 times faster than a racing car.

30 — 30 m/s: The Cheetah is the fastest animal. It runs faster than the national speed limit.

0 m/s

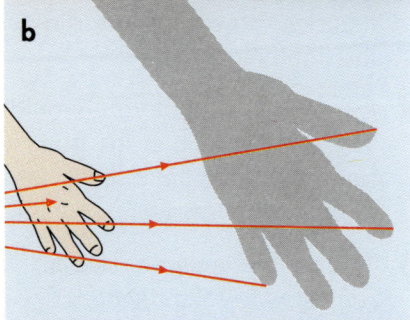

Picture 1 We will want to show the straight paths of light in diagrams. We do this using lines called **rays**.

Picture 2 The Sun's rays look straight.

6.2 As straight as …

The light from the Sun travels through space and passes into our eyes. That is why we can see the Sun.

We can see a light bulb in the same way. It sends light out in all directions. Wherever we stand, some of it passes into our eye and we detect it. We can only see something, if light comes off it and passes into our eyes.

However, most things don't make their own light. They are *lit up*. This page is lit up by the Sun or an electric light. The light strikes it and is **scattered** in all directions. Wherever you stand, some of this scattered light passes into your eye, so you can see the page.

You can only see things when there is a straight **line of sight**, between your eye and what you are looking at. This suggests that light travels in a straight line. You can check this. If you put your hand in between your eye and a lamp, you can no longer see the lamp. You have stopped the rays of light from the lamp reaching your eye.

We can show where light travels on a **ray diagram** (picture 1b). The paths of the rays of light are shown as straight lines with arrows. The arrows show which way the light is travelling. Remember a light ray passes **from** an object **to** your eye.

Can you see light rays?

On a sunny day you can sometimes see the Sun's rays coming into a dusty room. Do they look straight or curvy? This is more evidence that light travels in straight lines. You can only see the Sun's rays because the sunlight has been scattered by dust particles into your eyes. You can't really *see* rays of light.

You must never look directly at the Sun.

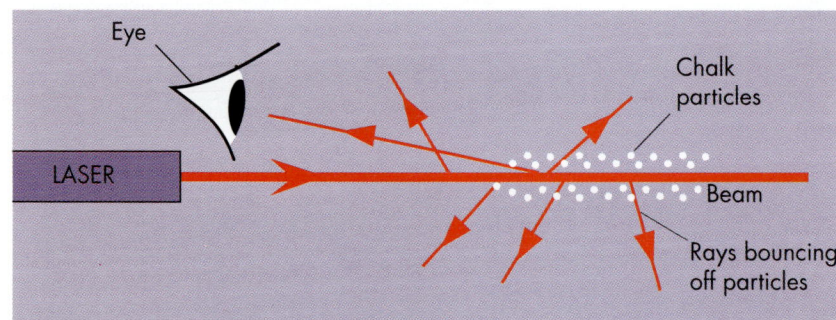

Picture 3 You can only see the path of a laser beam because some light is scattered by particles and passes into your eye.

A laser is a very special device. It sends out a highly concentrated beam of light in one direction. If you shine a laser at the wall you can see a spot of light. Does the beam seem to travel in a straight line? To see the path that the laser beam has followed, we need to sprinkle some chalk dust in the way. The light then bounces off the chalk particles and into our eyes.

Shadows

The light from a bulb lights up a whole room. However, if you put your hand in front of it you will get a shadow. The shadow is the same shape as your hand. Your hand has blocked out all the rays, which were going in that direction. The light which just missed your hand carried on in straight lines. That is why the shape of the shadow is the same as your hand.

Picture 4 The beam of laser light travels in a perfect straight line for a long way. A laser was used to make sure that the Channel Tunnel was dug in a straight line.

How can we get pictures?

In the **pinhole camera**, only one of the light rays from a point on an object passes through the pinhole. When this hits the screen you get an **image** of the object. One point on the object makes a spot at one point *only* on the screen. So you get a clear image. The points on an image are all in the right place. This is because a light ray from each point on the object has come in a straight line. It goes through the hole and hits the screen in the right place. The rays cross over, making the image upside down.

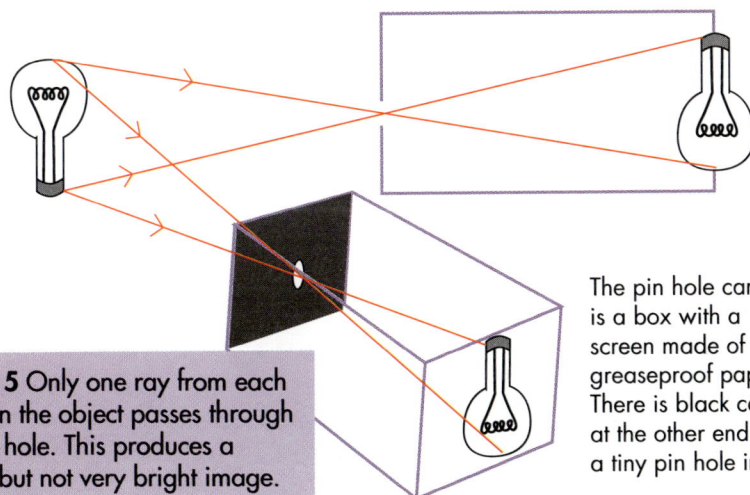

Picture 5 Only one ray from each point on the object passes through the pin hole. This produces a sharp, but not very bright image.

The pin hole camera is a box with a screen made of greaseproof paper. There is black card at the other end with a tiny pin hole in it.

QUESTIONS

1 How do we show the path of light in a diagram?

2 Can you actually *see* a light ray? Explain your answer.

3 We cannot see around corners. Explain why this adds to our idea that light travels in straight lines.

4 What would happen to shadows if light did *not* travel in a straight line?

5 Look at picture 1. If you were to move your hand closer to the bulb what would happen to the size of the shadow? Copy picture 1b and draw a similar diagram showing why the size of the shadow changes when you move your hand closer.

107

Picture 1 You see two cones. The real one is in front of the mirror and its reflection behind the mirror.

6.3 Lighting things up

We see some objects because they are lit up. The light that strikes them is scattered in all directions and some of this light passes into our eye. However, some surfaces do not scatter light in *all* directions.

One example is a mirror. When we look at a mirror, we don't see the surface of the mirror, we see **reflections** of other things. The reflection *looks* like it is on the other side of the mirror.

Why do we see reflections?

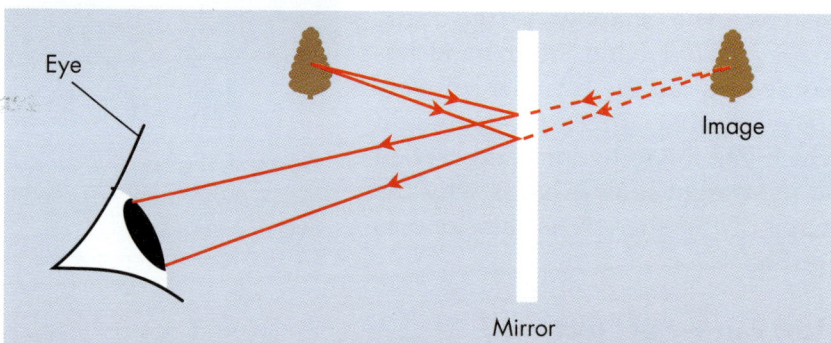

Picture 2 Your brain *thinks* that the light rays have come in a straight line. The dotted lines show where it thinks the rays have come from.

A mirror's surface is very flat, even under a microscope. The angle between an incoming light ray and the surface is always the same as the angle between the reflected ray and the surface (picture 2). All the light rays hitting a mirror's surface will do this. When these rays enter your eye, your brain is tricked. It *thinks* that the light must have travelled in a straight line. So it thinks that all the rays of light came from *behind* the mirror. That is why it *looks as though* there is a cone behind the mirror.

Although the surface of your desk *looks* flat, it is actually very bumpy under a microscope. So when light hits the surface, it bounces in all directions off the different edges – we say it is scattered. So you can't see reflections in the surface of your desk because the light is scattered in all different directions.

Picture 3 All the light rays bounce off the mirrored surface uniformly (**3a**). The rough surface scatters the rays in all different directions (**3b**).

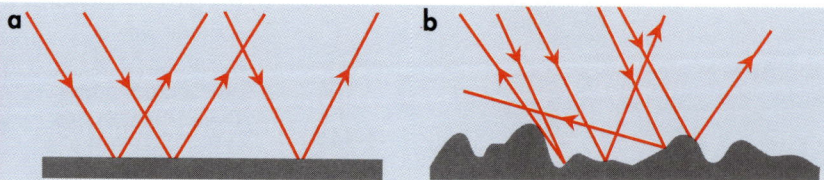

What happens with two mirrors?

Picture 5 How many people can fit in a changing room?

Have you ever been in a changing room of a clothes shop where they have two mirrors facing each other? How many reflections of yourself can you see? You can see a reflection of yourself in one mirror. There is a reflection of the reflection in the other mirror and a reflection of the reflection of the reflection in the first one again … and so it goes on.

If the mirrors are not facing each other you don't get so many reflections. This idea is used in a kaleidoscope. As well as making an interesting toy, a kaleidoscope can be used by designers for creating repeating or **symmetrical** patterns.

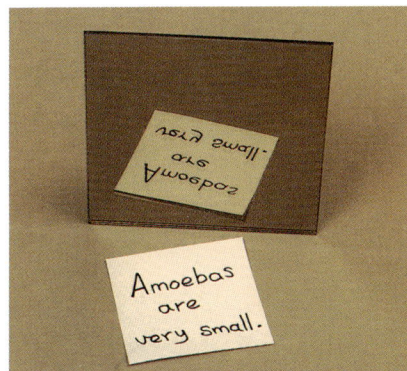

Picture 4 Mirror images are not exactly the same. Try writing your name so that it looks right in the mirror.

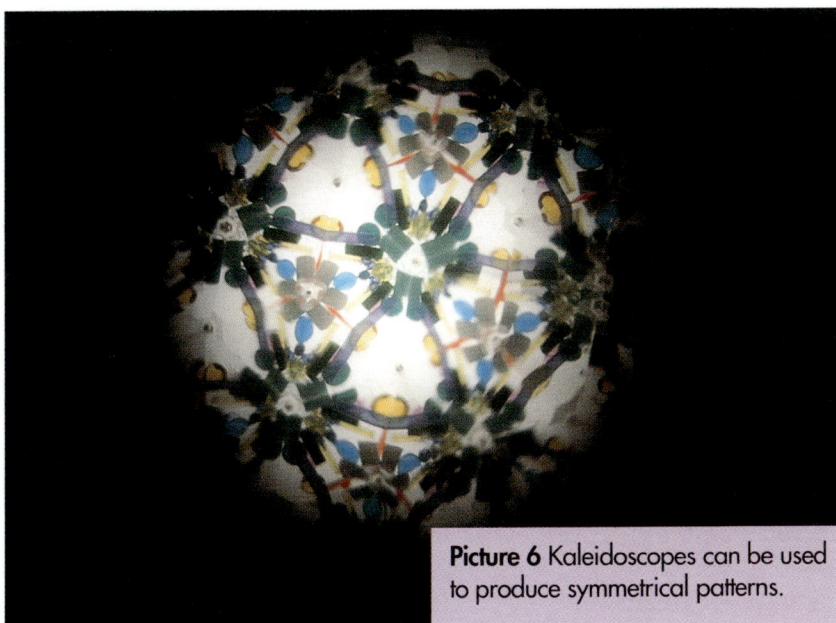

Picture 6 Kaleidoscopes can be used to produce symmetrical patterns.

What else can things do to light?

Some things neither scatter light nor reflect it. Light travels straight through. These materials are called **transparent**. You can see through them clearly.

If only one colour of light travels through something we call it a **filter**. For instance, a red filter only lets red light pass through it. Try looking at various coloured objects through different types of filter and see what happens to their colours.

QUESTIONS

1 When you look in a mirror, where is your image?

2 Explain what is meant by transparent.

3 Look around your house and list items which are
(a) transparent
(b) colour filters.
In each case say how this property makes them suitable for their job.

4 Look at a reflection of a friend in a mirror. It does not look quite the same as your friend. What is the difference?

5 You can see your reflection in a mirror, but you can't see your reflection in a white painted wall. Explain the difference.

6.4 Eyes and ears

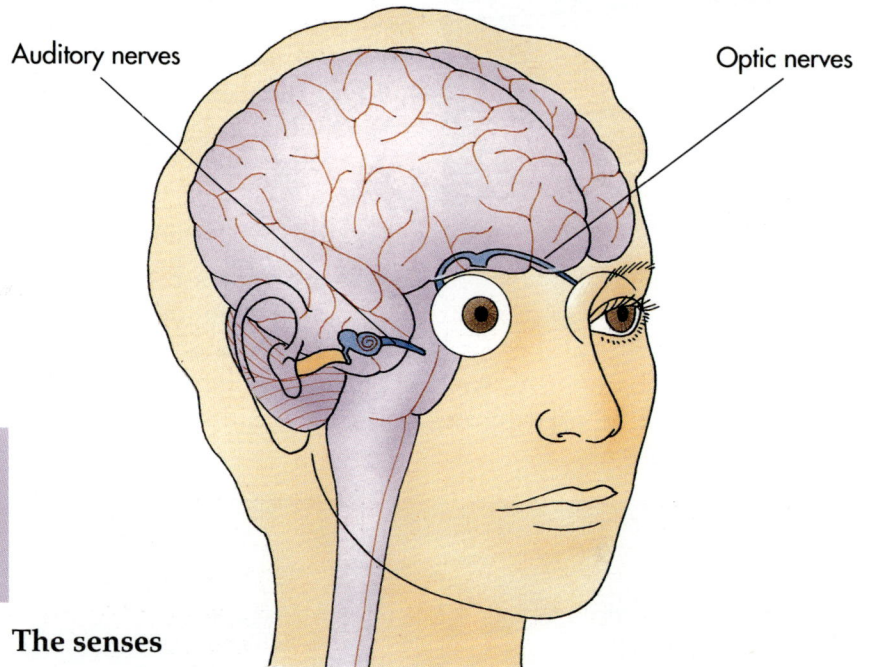

Auditory nerves

Optic nerves

Picture 1 The signals from our eyes are sent along **optic nerves** to the brain. The messages from our ears are sent along **auditory nerves** to the brain.

The senses

We have five main ways of finding out what is happening around us – seeing, hearing, tasting, smelling and touching. We call these our five main **senses**. We have special **sense organs** on our bodies for each one. We do have other senses – like the sense of balance.

Organs for seeing and hearing

Our eyes and ears are very complicated, clever detectors. They receive information about the outside World. But they are not the whole story. The hard work is done by the brain. Your brain uses signals sent by your eyes to build up pictures of your surroundings. Your brain also makes sense of the sounds that your ears receive. That is how we can talk to each other and enjoy music.

How clever are brains? Some scientists tried to trick their brains. They wore special spectacles which made everything seem upside down. However, their brains knew which way up the World *should* look! Within a day they saw everything the right way up again. Their brains had sorted out the muddle. What do you think happened when they *stopped* wearing the special spectacles?

The scientists had found out that although the eye detects the light from the outside World, it is the brain which makes sense of the signals.

Picture 2 Suppose you put on some upside down glasses. The World would look like this. Could you walk in it?

Two eyes

Picture 3 This is a two dimensional picture. You can tell that the car is coming closer to us. How?

Picture 4 To see the picture in 3-D, you will need to use a special pair of glasses. A red filter lets only the right view into the right eye and a green filter lets the left view into the left eye.

A picture in a book is flat – we say it has **2 dimensions** – height and width. We can only tell how far away things are in the picture by how big they look.

In reality we can judge distances very accurately. We manage this by having two eyes. Each eye sees an object from a slightly different angle. The brain uses these two different views to work out how far away the object is. The picture we see with two eyes has depth, as well as height and width. We say it has **3 dimensions**. We can see in 3-D because we have two eyes.

We can put 3-D pictures in a book, but we need to use two pictures (picture 4). One picture is the view that the right eye would normally have seen and the other picture is the view for the left eye. They are overlapped and the result is a bit strange.

Two ears

Many animals use their *ears* more than their eyes for finding things. Watch a cat or a dog when it hears a noise. It will move its ears to search it out, in the same way that you would take a *look* around. You need *two* ears to be able to tell where something is by listening.

Picture 5 If you want to see the World in 2 dimensions, try closing one eye. You will now find it hard to judge distance. If you don't believe this, almost stretch out your arms and try touching together the tips of a finger on each hand (still with only one eye open).

QUESTIONS

1 What do we call the parts of our body which detect the outside World?

2 When the scientists wore the funny spectacles, their brain knew which way up the World should be. Which other senses did it need to use?

3 How do we see in 3 dimensions?

4 What does the auditory nerve do?

5 Look at a cat, a horse and a flat fish. Make a note of where their eyes and ears are. Also describe how big these organs are. Why do you think they have developed like this?

111

6.5 Making music

Picture 1 We get great pleasure from music. We are very lucky to have the sense of hearing.

Picture 2 The tuning fork makes a sound but you cannot see it oscillating. You can show that a tuning fork is oscillating by putting it in some water.

Picture 3 You can see the movement of the guitar string, using a special photograph.

Picture 1 shows an orchestra. All of the instruments are making different musical sounds. How are these sounds produced? All the musicians have to put some effort into playing their instrument. They are blowing, bowing, striking or plucking. They have to do this to make part of the instrument move.

Sounds are made when something moves backwards and forwards quickly. We say it is **vibrating** or **oscillating**. For example, if the violinist plucks her violin string, the string will oscillate. You may not be able to *see* the string moving, but you would be able to feel it moving if you touched it.

How low can we go?

The instruments in the orchestra play different notes. Some will have a low **pitch** and some a high pitch. What decides the pitch of a note?

A higher note is produced by something which oscillates more often. We say that it has a higher **frequency** because the oscillations happen more frequently. We measure the frequency of a sound in **hertz** (Hz). This is the number of oscillations every second. A note with a frequency of 50 Hz would sound very low. A musician would say it had a low **pitch**. If the frequency were

100 Hz the note would sound higher. In fact it would be higher by an amount called an **octave**. Doubling the frequency makes that note an octave higher.

What makes a lower pitch note?

Picture 4 The larger tuning fork moves more slowly, so it makes a note with a lower pitch.

Picture 5 The piano keys are attached to hammers. These hit the strings and make them oscillate.

Picture 5 shows a grand piano. The long thick strings at the left-hand end make the low notes and the short strings at the other end make the high notes. The long thick strings are difficult to move, so they oscillate more slowly than the smaller strings. They produce a low note because the frequency of their oscillations is low.

When you blow over a milk bottle you can make a note. The note will be lower if there is less water in the bottle. It is the air in the bottle that is oscillating. When there is more air, the note produced is lower. If you look at a pipe organ you will see the different sizes of pipe. The longer pipes make the lower notes because there is more air in them.

Picture 6 The larger pipes make lower notes.

QUESTIONS

1 How are sounds made?

2 The *string* on a guitar oscillates to make the sound. What is oscillating for each of these
(a) a drum?
(b) a tuning fork?
(c) a milk bottle?
(d) an organ?
(e) your voice?

3 (a) What is meant by the frequency of a sound?
(b) What is the unit used to measure frequency?

4 A violin string playing middle C would make 256 complete oscillations every second (256 Hz). If another violin made a sound at 512 Hz, would this be a higher or lower note?

5 A piccolo is smaller than a flute. Do you think it will make higher or lower notes than a flute?

6.6 Musical tones

An orchestra always 'tunes up' before a concert. They all play the same note – it's called 'concert A'. They adjust their instruments to make sure that they are all at the same pitch. The frequency of all the instruments will be 440 Hz. But, although they are all playing the same frequency, no two instruments sound the same. Some of them will be louder than others, but also they will all have a slightly different **tone**.

Playing louder

If a musician wants to play an instrument more loudly, he or she will put more effort into it. For instance, a drummer would hit the drum harder and a trumpeter would blow harder. Suppose you twang a ruler on the bench. If you want to make a louder sound, what would you do? You would twang it harder or pull it down further before letting it go. This makes the size – or **amplitude** – of its oscillations larger (picture 1). The amplitude of an oscillation is a measure of its size. So a loud note has been made by an oscillation with a large amplitude.

Musical instruments oscillate very quickly (hundreds of times every second). This is too fast for us to see. We *can* see the way that an instrument oscillates by playing a note into a microphone and plugging this into an **oscilloscope** (picture 2). The oscilloscope plots a trace of the motion of the instrument. The oscilloscope can plot things which move faster than our eyes can see.

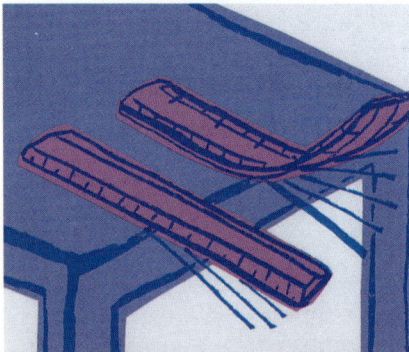

Picture 1 The amplitude tells us the size of the oscillation. The bigger the amplitude, the louder the sound.

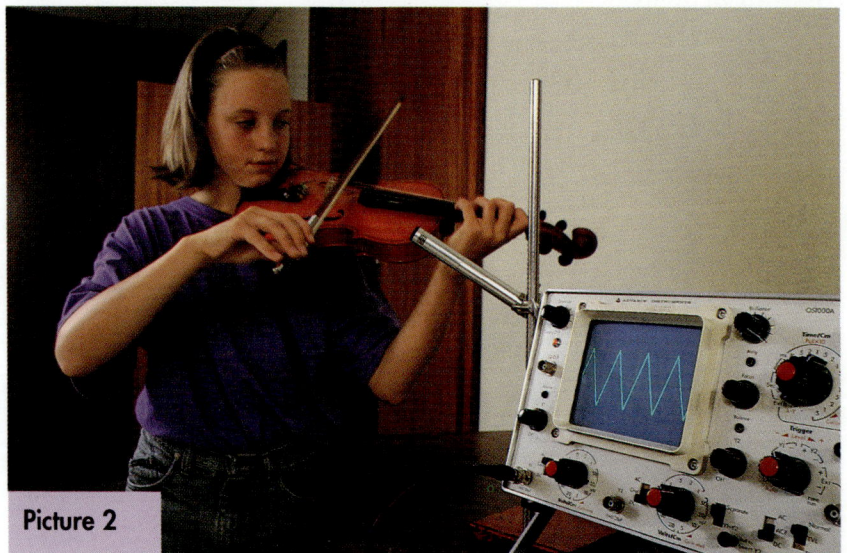

Picture 2

Tones

All the instruments in the orchestra have a different tone or character, even when they are playing the same note. The sound that they make depends on the type of instrument, how well it is made and how well it is played. This will decide the way in which it oscillates. A tuning fork makes a very pure note. Picture 3a shows the oscilloscope trace of a tuning fork. It is a smooth curve. We call it a **simple harmonic**. If you look at the trace for a violin, you will see that there are extra shapes on the curve. These make the instrument sound less like a tuning fork. The frequency is still the same because the whole pattern (a complete oscillation) is repeated the same number of times every second.

Synthesizers

People use synthesizers to make sounds which are like real instruments. In this case it is an electronic circuit which makes the oscillations. If the synthesizer is to sound exactly like a violin, the trace (picture 3e) should be the same as a violin's trace (picture 3d). However, you can see that, although the trace is very similar, it is not exactly the same. The tone of a violin is very complicated and, therefore, difficult to imitate.

Picture 3

a The tuning fork makes a pure note. This shows up as a smooth curve on the oscilloscope.

b The higher pitched tuning fork has a higher frequency. So the trace goes up and down more often.

c This tuning fork has been hit harder and is making a louder sound. The amplitude of the trace is larger.

d The violin does not make such a pure note. The tone of the violin leads to a very complicated trace.

e The synthesizer cannot make a sound *exactly* the same as the violin. The synthesizer would sound very similar to a violin, but not perfect.

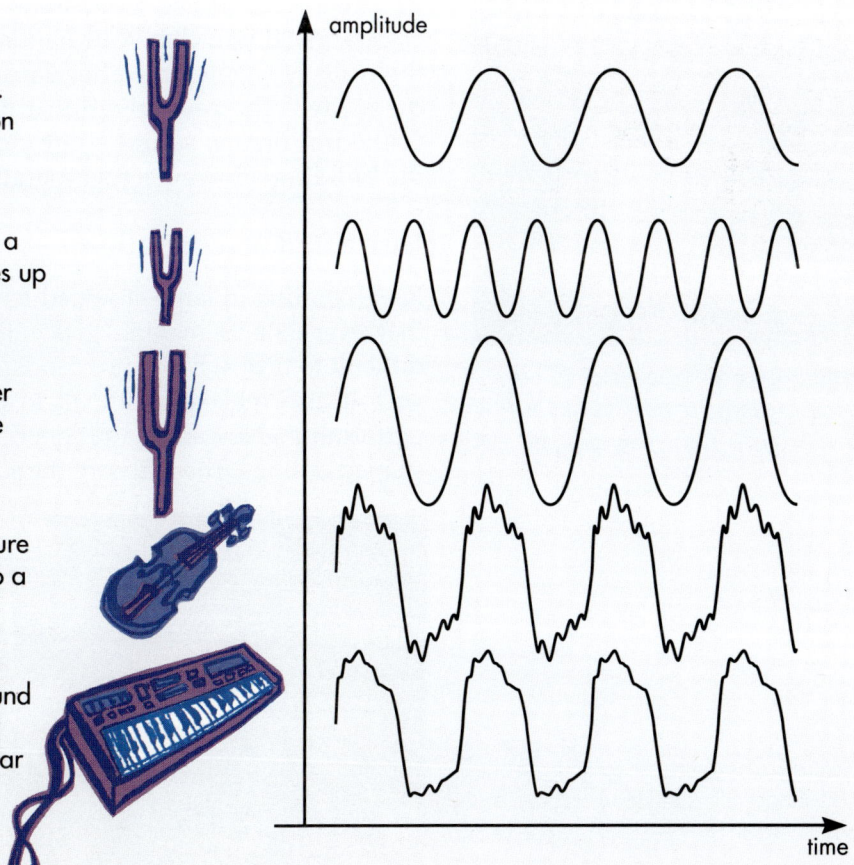

6.7 Loud and clear

Can we reflect sound?

Sometimes when you make a loud noise outside you get an **echo**. The sound has been reflected, usually off a wall.

If you are fifty metres from a wall it will take about a third of a second for the sound to travel to the wall, bounce off it and travel back again.

Lots of echoes

You only get good clear echoes when you are outside. Inside a building the sound keeps bouncing off all the walls. This is a bit like all those millions of reflections you get with two mirrors facing each other. However, sound travels much more slowly than light. It will take longer to bounce off some walls than others. So the sound gets all mixed up – you cannot hear a clear echo. Instead the sound **reverberates**.

Reverberation is very obvious in large stone buildings, like cathedrals. If you clap your hands the sound keeps bouncing off all the walls for some time afterwards. The time it takes for a sound to die away – the **reverberation time** – can be more than a second. Cathedral organs sound so grand because of the reverberation of the building. However, reverberation is not always a good thing.

Unwanted reverberation

Reverberation in large crowded halls can be a problem. All the noise that everyone is making gets reflected everywhere. This makes it difficult to hear what your friends are saying, even if they are close to you. It also makes it difficult to hear musicians or actors who are performing. Nowadays designers use soft materials and specially shaped ceilings. These absorb the sound and reduce the reverberation.

Picture 1 A single wall gives a clear echo when a sound bounces off it. Inside a building, the sound bounces off all the different walls at different times. This is what causes **reverberation**.

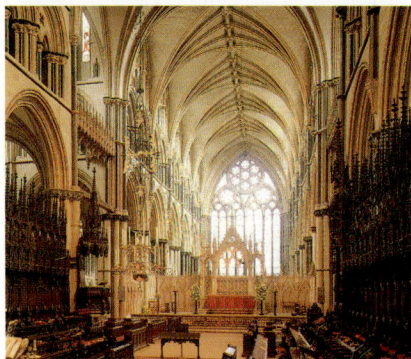

Picture 2 Large stone buildings have a lot of reverberation. This makes church music sound very grand.

Picture 3 Designers use special materials and shapes of ceiling to absorb the sound and **dampen** the effects of reverberation.

Have you ever had trouble understanding an announcement in a railway station? The problem is reverberation. It is worst if a single loudspeaker is used. This has to be loud enough to be heard everywhere. The words then bounce off all the different walls and become a blur of sound. This can be improved by using lots of small speakers.

Picture 4 Lots of small speakers are used to cut down on reverberation on platforms.

Special effects

When you listen to the radio or watch television, most of the action has taken place in a studio. The studio can be made to sound like any real place, like the middle of a field or a large cathedral. The sound engineers can change the shape and material of the studio using screens and curtains. But they cannot make it bigger. However, they can make it *sound* bigger by adding their own reverberation electronically.

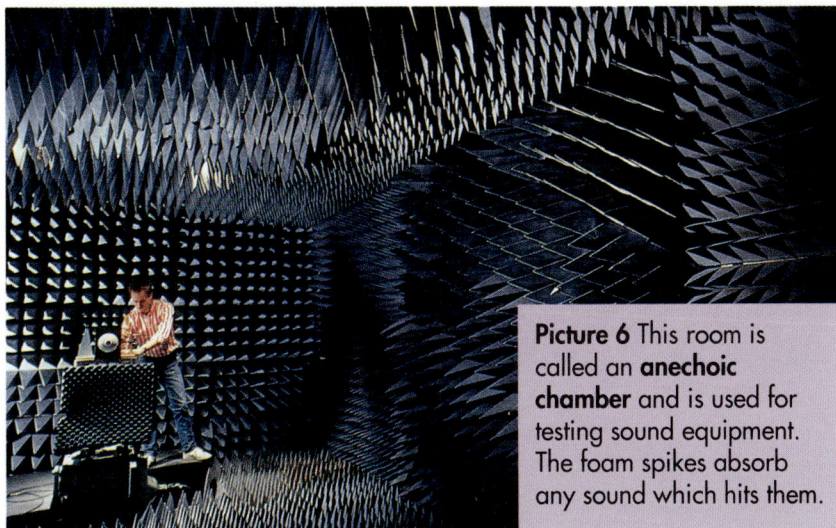

Picture 6 This room is called an **anechoic chamber** and is used for testing sound equipment. The foam spikes absorb any sound which hits them.

Picture 5 The radio programme 'The Archers' is all recorded in one studio. The screens are moved to change the reverberation of the studio. It is made to sound like a living room, a barn or the farmyard.

QUESTIONS

1 What is an echo?

2 As you move further from a wall, what will happen to the time you have to wait for the echo?

3 New airports use lots of small speakers to make their announcements, rather than one big speaker. How does this help people hear the message?

4 (a) Give an example of unwanted reverberation.
(b) How can this be reduced?

5 How can a radio studio be made to *sound like*
(a) a field?
(b) a cathedral?

Expansion to see particles (X million million million times)

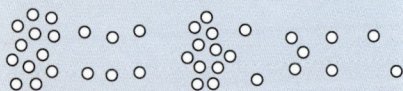

Picture 1 The air particles move backwards and forwards. They bump into each other to pass on the sound wave. This is similar to the coils on a slinky carrying a pulse.

Picture 2 a The train is making a lot of noise on the track. The sound carries along the track …

Picture 3 Rabbits warn each other of danger by thumping the ground. The sound carries well through the ground.

6.8 Long distance messages

Talking

When you talk to someone nearby the sound is carried in the air. When there is no air, we call it a **vacuum**. Sound does not travel through a vacuum, so if there were no air your friend would not be able to hear you. All matter is made up of tiny particles, and these particles carry the sound. Air particles carry our sound message by moving backwards and forwards, bouncing into each other. This flow of sound energy is a type of **wave** – a **sound wave**.

Ear to the ground

Although we can hear someone who is close to us, once they get further away it is hard to hear them even when they shout.

Solid things carry sound better and further than air. The sound cannot easily escape from the solid. A railway track will carry the sound of a train for many kilometres. The ground can also carry sounds. This is used by rabbits to warn their friends of danger. When one rabbit thumps the ground, the whole colony gets the message.

Solids are also made up from tiny particles. They are much closer together than the gas particles, often in a regular pattern. A sound wave can be carried along this arrangement.

Picture 2 b … and can be heard some distance away. **Do not try this yourself, as it is dangerous to go near railway lines.**

When any particle is vibrated, it will pass on the same movement to the next one, and then the next one and so on until the message reaches the other end.

Underwater

Picture 4 Dolphins send sound through the water. The sound carries a very long way.

Picture 5 Sailors use **sounding** to find the depth of the sea.

Sound also carries well in liquids like water. Dolphins make sounds which carry for many kilometres underwater.

Sailors bounce a sound off the bottom of the sea to find out how deep it is. They measure the time for the echo to return. From this they can work out how far the sound travels there and back. This tells them the depth. The method is called **sounding**.

Seeing with sound

Bats cannot see at all well. However, they can fly quickly through caves without crashing into the walls. They can even catch tiny, fast moving insects in mid flight. How can they do this without good eyesight? They do it by using sound.

Bats have developed a method called **echolocation**. They send out a series of little pulses of **ultrasound**. This is a sound which is too high for us to hear. Then they listen for the **echoes** to **locate** any object. The pulses are sent out so rapidly that they can even detect an insect.

Now you may think 'That's incredible – the bat has to listen to lots of little pulses of sound and then work out where the cave walls and the insect are'.

It is amazing, but easy for a bat. The bat's brain turns the pattern of echoes into a picture. This is no more complicated than what we do when we see things using light. A bat 'sees' things using sound.

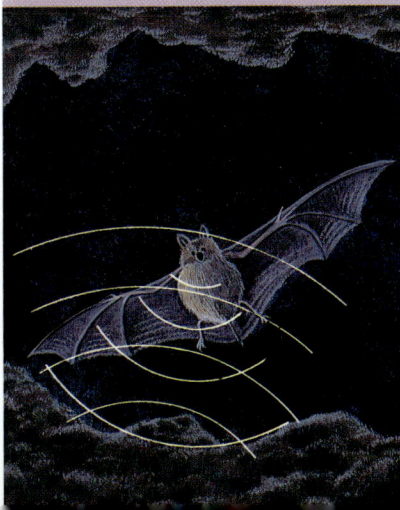

Picture 6 Bats use echolocation to find their way around.

QUESTIONS

1 Why does sound *not* travel in a vacuum?

2 What is a sound wave?

3 Gas particles are further apart than particles in a solid. Why do you think sound travels better in a solid?

4 In water sound travels 1500 metres in a second. A sailor is **sounding** to find the depth of water. How deep is the water if the time for an echo is
   (a) 1 second?
   (b) 2 seconds?
   (c) 0.5 seconds?

5 Find out about ultrasound. What is it and what is it used for?

6 Why do you think bats do not use their eyes very much?

119

6.9 How does the ear work?

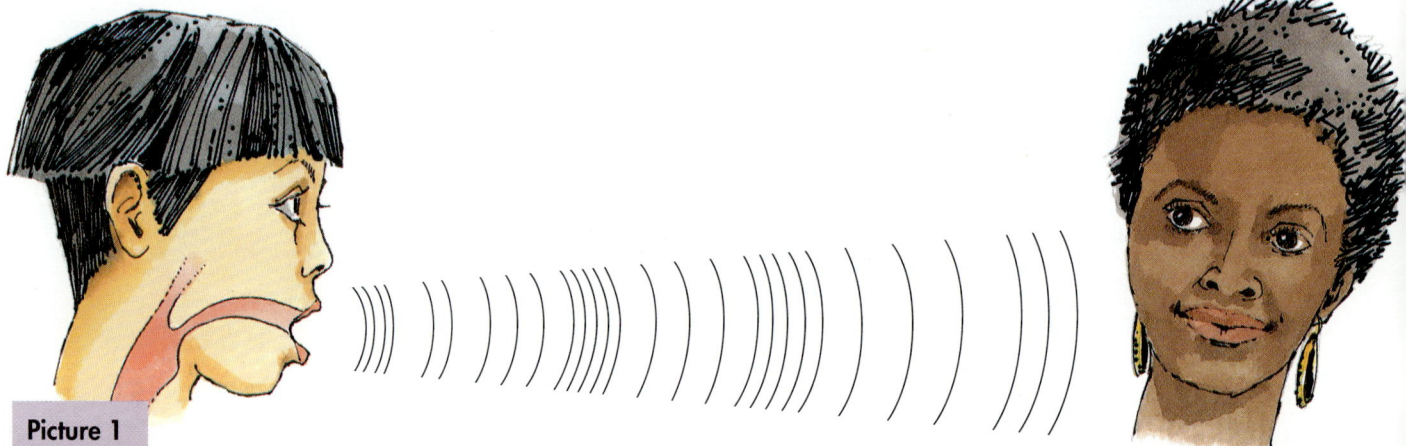

Picture 1

Kyoko makes words in her throat and mouth. Her vocal chords vibrate to produce a sound. The sound is then shaped by the movement of her mouth to form the words. The sound wave is carried by the air and reaches Karen. Let's see how Karen detects the sound wave that reaches her.

Your ear

Most of your ear is inside your head. It has three main areas – **the outer ear**, **the middle ear** and **the inner ear**. The sound wave is collected in the outer ear. It is made stronger in the middle ear. It is turned into electrical messages in the inner ear. These electrical messages are then sent along a nerve to the brain.

What you can see?

The part of the ear which you can see on the side of your head is called the **pinna**. It helps to collect the sound wave, which travels down to the **eardrum**. This is like a drum skin stretched across the tube. The eardrum vibrates in time with the moving air of the sound wave.

The middle ear

The middle ear has three small bones (**ear-bones**) which **amplify** the sound, making it about twenty times stronger. There is a tube from the middle ear to the back of the throat called the **eustachian tube**. This only opens when the pressure on the outside changes suddenly. The eustachian tube lets air through to change the pressure on the

Picture 2 Animals can move their pinnae to help them hear where a sound is coming from. They can also hear sounds which are too high for us.

120

inside as well. You may have noticed this when your ears 'pop' when you go up in a lift or go through a railway tunnel.

Messages to the brain

The last ear-bone is joined to the **oval window** which seals off the inner ear. When this vibrates it makes the liquid inside the inner ear vibrate inside the **cochlea**. Little hairs in the cochlea detect the sounds and send electrical messages to the brain. The hairs are all different lengths to pick up the different pitches of sound. The shortest hairs pick up the highest pitches. Your brain can tell the pitch and tone of a sound from the messages sent by the cochlea.

Your cochlea cannot detect all sounds. The lowest frequency that it picks up is about 30 Hz, and the highest frequency is about 20 000 Hz. Any vibration with a higher frequency is called **ultrasound**. Different people have different ranges of hearing.

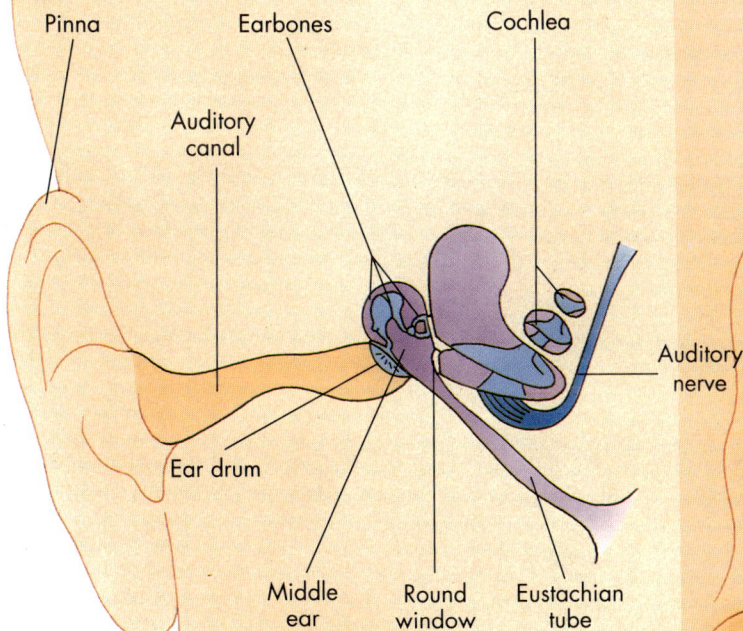

Pinna   Earbones   Cochlea

Auditory canal

Auditory nerve

Ear drum

Middle ear   Round window   Eustachian tube

Picture 3

QUESTIONS

1 What are the three main areas of the ear?

2 What happens to the sound in the middle ear?

3 What happens to the sound in the inner ear?

4 Name two differences when a dog's hearing is compared with a human's.

5 Explain what happens when your ears go 'pop' when you go up in a lift.

6.10 Treat your neighbour as you would like to be treated

Unwanted noise

Picture 1 The airport can build a **blast shield** between the runway and houses. This shield stops the noise having a straight path from the noisy aeroplanes to the houses.

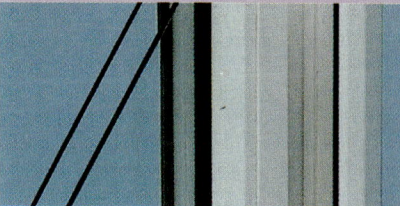

Picture 2 Double glazing reduces the noise inside a house. The two pieces of glass with an air gap between them don't let as much sound through as a single piece of glass.

Sound allows us to communicate and enjoy ourselves. However, unwanted sounds can pollute our surroundings. They can even be harmful. You can nearly always hear some unwanted noise, but often it is possible to ignore it.

People who live near airports cannot ignore the noise that the aeroplanes make. It is very loud indeed and it doesn't stop. A plane takes off from Heathrow Airport, in London, every thirty seconds. The power needed to make it lift off is enormous and this produces a lot of noise. There are ways of reducing the noise, but it is still very loud.

A scale of sound

The loudness of sound is measured in **decibels** (dB). Very loud sounds are damaging because they make the eardrum move too violently. A sound of 130 dB is painful. If the level reaches 150 dB, it will probably break a bone in your ear or burst your eardrum.

Picture 3 It is important for people who work with noisy machinery to wear earmuffs.

Constant noise

Noisy factories are a big problem. The sound level may be much less than 130 dB, but the people who work there have to put up with the noise all the time. This can lead to deafness, if they do not protect their ears.

Listening to loud music a lot can damage your ears. This is even more harmful if the music is fed straight into your ears using headphones.

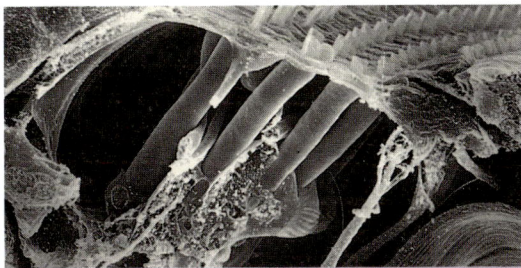

Picture 4 The hair cells on the cochlea are very small and sensitive. If they are damaged by noise, they do not regrow.

Table 1 The loudness of sounds is measured in decibels.		
	210	
	200	
Rocket taking off (close by)	190	VERY VERY LOUD
	180	
	170	
	160	
Bones in ear may be broken	150	
	140	
Pain begins	130	Jet aircraft (30 m away)
Road drill (1 m away)	120	Rock group
World record for shouting	110	
	100	Howling baby (1 m away)
	90	Passing train (25 m away)
Inside a small car	80	Loud radio
Inside a large shop	70	
Inside a busy office	60	Telephone conversation
Normal conversation	50	Quiet street
Quiet conversation	40	Birds singing
	30	Library reading room
Soft whisper	20	
Falling leaf	10	very very quiet
Threshold of hearing	0	

Deafness

Eight million people in Britain have hearing difficulties and 50 000 of these have no useful hearing at all.

Picture 5 People who are born deaf find it very difficult to learn to speak. They rely on sign language or lip reading to communicate, even more than other deaf people.

Tinnitus is a common problem for older people who have had to put up with a lot of noise. A fault in the cochlea makes a constant ringing sound in their ears. It can be relieved with a device which fits behind the ear. This masks the ringing sound heard by the sufferer.

The inner ear can be damaged by loud noise or by catching a nasty disease, such as meningitis. This **sensory** deafness cannot usually be cured.

Problems in the middle ear stop the message being carried from the eardrum to the oval window. Often this **conductive deafness** can be relieved by using a hearing aid and can actually be cured by doctors.

QUESTIONS

1 What sound would be likely to cause pain?

2 What can cause sensory deafness?

3 Why do you think people are particularly upset by noise from crying babies, late night parties and snorers?

4 Why is it not sensible to listen to too much loud music, while you are young?

5 Imagine you live near Heathrow Airport. What could you say to the airport manager to persuade him to reduce noise produced by aeroplanes?

123

Helping the deaf

There are eight million people in Britain with hearing difficulties and 50 000 of these have no useful hearing at all. Most of these people rely on lip reading to understand what people are saying. Here are some ways that you can help people understand you when they cannot hear you well. Read through them carefully then answer the questions at the end.

If you meet someone with a hearing difficulty:

A keep calm and treat the person as normally as possible.

B make sure you have their attention.

C do **not** shout. It is a common reaction, but does not help. It only causes embarrassment.

D speak slowly and carefully, but do not distort your face.

E face towards the person you are speaking to. Try to face the light as well.

F cut out as much background noise as possible.

G do not drink, eat or do anything else that involves putting your hand in front of your face. Lip readers must be able to see your mouth.

H use plain language. Many words look the same to lip readers. The more common the word, the better – they will be more used to seeing it spoken.

I if they don't seem to understand, try rephrasing what you are saying.

J write things down if you think it is necessary. Again, it is easier if you use common and quite short words.

K if the deaf person is with a friend, make sure you talk to the deaf person. The friend will still be able to hear what you are saying, and help if needed.

We laugh at Basil Fawlty because he behaves in exactly the wrong way. He exaggerates all the mistakes. But try to imagine how the deaf Colonel felt.

QUESTIONS

1 Why should you not drink or eat when you are talking to a deaf person?

2 How should you speak to a deaf person?

3 What is a common reaction to deaf people? Why should you avoid it?

4 Why should you not use long words?

5 You are standing in front of a window in a dark room, having a cup of coffee and watching the TV. A deaf friend comes into the room. What would you do before you spoke to her?

6 Imagine being a deaf person walking into a busy shop with a friend. The assistant does not follow suggestions A, B, C, D and J. Describe what you think it would be like.

7 Think of some pairs of words which sound the same. For example, 'bill' and 'pill'. Get a friend to mouth them to you and see if you can tell the difference.

Index

acceleration 88, 89; see also free fall
acid 74, 82, 83
adaptation 22
air pressure 76
air resistance 93
alloys 52–3
animals 28–31
apparatus 2–3

babies 46
Bacon, Roger 6
bacteria 28, 68, 69, 75
balloon 12–13
Beaufort scale 77
beetles, and hedges 49
blood groups 27
brain 110–11, 120–1
brick 56
brine (salt water) 61

camera 107
camouflage 23
car crash 96–7
cells 36–7
change
    in the world 20–1
    to weather 80–1
chemical change 55
chemical weathering 57
chlorophyll 32
classification 28–33
clouds 78, 79
coal 54–5, 58–9
conifers 33
controls 14, 15

deafness 123, 124
decibel 122–3
difference 34–5
distillation 62–3, 65
dowsing 15

ear 111, 120–1
echo 116–17
elastic force 90, 91
embryo 45
energy, for animals 38
estimation 25
experiments 9, 16, 100–1
    design 14–15, 17
eye 37, 110–11
eye protection 4

Faraday, Michael 8–9
features, for sorting groups 26–7
ferns 32
filtering 62, 74
fire precautions 4–5
flowering plants 32, 33
flying 12–13
food 32, 38
force
    and acceleration 88, 89
    and injury 94–7
    measurement 91
forces 87, 90–1; see also gravity
fossil fuel: see coal; oil
    and global warming 80, 81
free–fall 92–3, 101
friction 86–7, 93

Galileo Galilei 100
gas 70
gravity 90, 92, 98–101, 100–1
greenhouse effect 80–1
growth 38, 39

habitat 24–5
hedge 48–9
hertz 112
Hertz, Heinrich 16–17

images 107, 108, 109
inference 17
inheritance 22, 34
injury 94–7
invertebrates 30–1
iron ore 55

keys 26–7, 33
kingdoms 28

laser 106, 107
life cycle 42
life process 38–9
light, speed of 105
light rays 106–7; see also mirrors
limestone 55, 57
liquid 70, 119

magnifying glass 6
mass 88, 89, 98

materials 50–3
    for building 56–7
    from the earth 54–5
    history 52
menstrual cycle 42–3
metals 50, 52
microbes 75
microscope 6–7
minerals 54
mining, coal 58–9
mirrors 108–9
mixtures 62–3
molluscs 30
Montgolfier brothers 12–13
movement 38, 39

Newton, Isaac 98
newton (N) 88, 91
noise 122–3
notes, pitch of 112–13
nylon 67

observation 9, 10, 17
oil 64–5
organs 37
oscillation 112, 114
ovaries 40, 41, 42

petrochemicals 64
pH 74
pitch 112
planets 10, 99
plants 32–3
plastics 50, 65, 66
pollution
    by noise 122–3
    of ponds 82–3
polythene 65, 66
ponds 82–3
prediction 18, 20
pregnancy 44–5
puberty 40
purification
    salt 61
    water 68–9, 72

rain 72, 73, 78–9
raw materials 51
ray diagram 106
reflections, in mirrors 108–9
reproduction 38, 39, 44–6
reservoir 69, 73

reverberation 116–17
rocks 54, 55, 56, 60

safety 4–5, 94–5
salt 60–1
sampling 25
sea water 60, 61
seat belts 96–7
senses 110–11
sensitivity 38, 39
sex organs 41
similarity 34–5, 49
slipping 86–7
Solar System 11, 99
solid 70, 118
Somerville, Mary 10
sorting 26–7
sound 112–19, 104
sound wave 118–19
speed 77, 84–5
sperm 40, 41, 42
states of matter 70
stone, building 56
survival 21, 22–3

telekinesis 14
telepathy 14
temperature 29, 77
tinnitus 123
tones 114–15
transparency 109

vacuum 105, 118
variables 14, 16, 17
vertebrates 29

water, testing purity 74–5
water cycle 72, 78
water purification 68–9, 72
weather, and greenhouse effect 80–1
weather forecast 20
weather front 78–9
weathering 57
weight 98
wind 76–7